COME

and

GET IT!

recipes to warm the heart
& satisfy the soul

KAREN EHMAN
New York Times Bestselling Author

MACEY EHMAN LPC, NCC

To my daughter-in-love, Mariange. I couldn't have hand-picked a more beautiful soul to love, partner with, care for, and especially cook for our son, Spencer. Our family's life is sweeter now because we have you.

Karen

To my Mommie and my Granny Brewer, and in memory of my Mema. Your prayers have carried me thus far and y'all have made me into the woman and cook that I am today. All my love and gratitude.

Macey

Hi Friend,

We are so thrilled that you now hold in your hands our very first cookbook, hot off the presses! We are a mother-in-law and daughter-in-law team who loves to cook. I, (Karen), met Macey when she started following me on Instagram after reading one of my books and doing its corresponding Bible study. While following me, she connected with my son, Mitchell. Soon an online, long-distance friendship grew into true love and they married the following year. With that nuptial, a Midwestern Mama gained a very Southern daughter-in-law.

Instead of falling into the pattern many families have—where the mother-in-law and daughter-in-law compete with each other—we decided to collaborate instead! This book is a result of that collaboration, which really was a labor of love. In this resource, you will find over 140 recipes that our loved ones gobble up. Some have been used for decades by Karen. Some are brand new to Macey's growing family.

The two of us have very different personalities. Karen is talkative and outgoing. Macey is contemplative and quiet. We also have language differences due to the parts of the country in which we were raised. For example, Macey says, "Hey, y'all!" while Karen quips "Hi, you guys!" Macey calls the thing you put groceries in at the supermarket a buggy. Karen refers to it as a bascart. (Yes, you read that right. It is a term her father acquired when he worked for the Kroger company in the 1950's that means a combination of a basket and a shopping cart. Hey, it's in the dictionary!) And we simply won't ever agree on the proper way to pronounce pecan or caramel. (Is it PEE-can or puh-KAHN? CAR-muhl or CARE-uh-mel?)

But one thing we do both agree on is that we love to cook for and care for our families. And we aren't the first generation to feel this way! You will see many recipes tucked within these pages from our ancestors and other relatives who are still living. We also desire to use our kitchens and homes as places where we can do as the Bible commands—offer hospitality to others. First Peter 4:9 says, "Offer hospitality to one another without grumbling." Often, we grumble because we just don't know what to serve our guests! We pray this cookbook offers you lots of recipes, hospitality hacks, and soul-soothing thoughts to ponder that will assist you in your quest to make your home a haven for others when they visit.

Are you ready? Flip through these pages. Find a recipe you'd like to try. Fill up your buggy—or your bascart—with the needed ingredients, buying organic if you can. Fire up the oven and whip out the needed pots and pans. You'll be cooking for a crowd in no time, calling out to all those you love within earshot, *"Come and get it!"*

Thank you for the joy and honor of sharing our most treasured family heirloom recipes with you.

With Midwestern love and Southern grace,

Karen & Macey

DRESSINGS, DIPS & SEASONINGS | 217

ABOUT THE AUTHORS | 230

APPETIZERS&
BEVERAGES

"Nowadays, people are so jeezled up. If they took some chamomile tea and spent more time rocking on the porch in the evening listening to the liquid song of the hermit thrush, they might enjoy life more."

— TASHA TUDOR

Hospitality doesn't always need to include serving your guests an entire meal. Having others over to eat appetizers and drink something hot and creamy—or cool and refreshing—can make for a wonderful time of connection. Here are some of our go-to hors d'oeuvres and beverages for you to try.

HOMEMADE PUMPKIN SPICE LATTE

Karen

My late mother absolutely loved pumpkin spice lattes. Whichever one of us saw the first pumpkin spice latte each fall—signifying that PSL season had arrived—would text the other one and simply say, "It's here!" I miss her every autumn when pumpkin spice season rolls around. Thankfully, my daughter and both daughters-in-law also love this hot and creamy drink, so now I can enjoy it with them. Here is a delicious homemade version for you to try.

PREP TIME · 10 minutes

- 3 tablespoons pumpkin purée
- ¾ teaspoon pumpkin pie spice, plus more for serving
- 3 tablespoons sugar (extra-fine sugar, if possible)
- 1 tablespoon vanilla extract
- 3 cups whole milk, warmed
- ½ cup hot strong coffee or espresso
- Whipped cream for topping

INSTRUCTIONS

1   Place all the ingredients, except for the coffee, into a blender. (You can also use a large measuring cup or bowl and a hand-held milk frother.) Blend until smooth.

2   Pour the hot coffee into the blender and blend again until it's all well-incorporated, about 2 minutes.

3   Pour the drink into two cups and garnish with whipped cream and additional pumpkin spice, if desired.

4   Store any leftovers in an airtight jar with a lid. It will last about 24 to 48 hours in the fridge.

Substitutes: For best results, use whole milk. You can use almond, soy, or coconut milk but the result will be a thinner latte.

YIELDS · 2-3 servings

COZY LONDON FOG

Macey

It has always been on my bucket list to travel to London and the United Kingdom. So far, my feet have remained planted firmly on US soil, but when my heart wants to travel across the pond, I fix a cup of London fog. Pair this with a Harry Potter movie marathon or a good book (like the Harry Potter series, The Chronicles of Narnia *series, or the* Mary Poppins *series), and you've got a recipe for an amazing night in (or "day" if you are sensitive to caffeine)!*

PREP TIME · 10 minutes

- 8 ounces hot water
- 1 Earl Grey tea bag
- 8 ounces whole milk
- ½ teaspoon vanilla extract
- ¼ teaspoon lavender extract (optional)
- 1 tablespoon maple syrup

INSTRUCTIONS

1 Boil 8 ounces of water.

2 Steep your tea bag for 3 to 5 minutes, as desired.

3 Froth milk, vanilla extract, lavender extract, and maple syrup in a large container.

4 Pour frothed mixture into your tea, stir, and enjoy!

YIELDS · 2 servings

ALICIA'S ICED MAPLE LATTE

Macey

This recipe is named after my best friend, Alicia, who is always down to grab a cup of coffee from the local coffee shop whenever I come to town! She most often orders an iced latte of some kind, and her drink orders inspired this recipe. As I think back on all of my close relationships, I have such fond memories of sipping a cup of coffee with my parents, grandparents, dear friends, and in-laws. On front porches, in living rooms with music drifting by, in the heat of summer, or with a snowfall just outside my window—perfect no matter the circumstances!

PREP TIME · 5 minutes plus 2 hours cooling time

- ¾ cup brewed coffee of choice
- ¼ cup ice
- ¾ cup whole milk (or alternative)
- ¼ cup maple syrup
- 32-ounce jar with lid

INSTRUCTIONS

1   Brew your desired coffee. I love Decaf Caramel Creme from Schuil's in Grand Rapids, Michigan because it turns this amazing drink into an iced caramel maple coffee!

2   Once brewed, put in your refrigerator to cool.

3   When your coffee has cooled, pour ¾ cup of coffee into a 32-ounce jar.

4   Add ¼ cup of ice and ¾ cup of whole milk or a milk alternative.

5   Next, add ¼ cup of pure maple syrup, adding gradually and tasting periodically so that you do not over-sweeten your coffee (I like mine sweet, but this may be too much for some people so add to taste).

6   Stir and enjoy!

YIELDS · 2-4 servings

Hospitality Hack

If you have extra brewed coffee, pour it into a silicone ice cube mold and put it in your freezer. Add these to your iced coffee so that as the coffee ice cubes melt, they make your coffee stronger and not watered down! If you're like us when chatting with friends, our coffee goes unattended at times, and this is the perfect solution!

PEPPERMINT MOCHA *Hot, Please*

Macey

I love Christmas time for so many reasons, but enjoying a peppermint mocha is one of my absolute favorite Christmas pastimes. What I don't love is all of the harmful ingredients found in most lattes that you order from a restaurant or coffee shop. So, I tasked myself with making my own! Grab your favorite mug, follow the steps below, and enjoy a warm mug of deliciousness—perhaps by a crackling fire! Sprinkle finely crushed candy canes on top for the deluxe version.

PREP TIME · 5 minutes

COOK TIME · 5 minutes

- 1 cup brewed hot coffee
- 1 cup whole milk
- 1 tablespoon cacao powder
- 3 tablespoons sugar
- ¼ teaspoon peppermint extract
- ¼ teaspoon vanilla extract
- Whipped cream for topping
- Crushed candy canes (optional)

SOUL SOOTHER

Watching flames in a fireplace can be very therapeutic and even beneficial for our vision. Further, it can help us empty our minds and promote relaxation by reducing blood pressure. I would recommend going one step further and filling your mind with things that are true, noble, right, pure, lovely, admirable, excellent, and praiseworthy (Philippians 4:8). Thus, there are positive impacts, not only to your physical vision, but your spiritual vision as well!

INSTRUCTIONS

1 Brew your desired coffee.

2 In a small saucepan, add milk, cacao powder, and sugar. Heat on medium heat until small bubbles begin to form, and the sugar has dissolved.

3 Stir in your coffee, peppermint extract, and vanilla extract.

4 Remove from heat.

5 Serve in your favorite mug with whipped cream or your desired toppings! Best served with friends!

YIELDS · 2 servings

BASIL LIMEADE

Karen

You might not think basil belongs in a sweet summer drink, but trust me. This is delicious! A copycat recipe I created after visiting an eatery near my daughter Kenna's home in Charlotte, NC. Very unique, earthy, and refreshing. You can also float some blueberries on top for a fun garnish.

PREP TIME · 10 minutes
COOK TIME · 5 minutes

- 5 cups water, divided
- 1 cup sugar
- ¼ cup fresh basil leaves, coarsely chopped
- 1½ cups fresh lime juice (10 to 12 limes)
- 1 lime, sliced and seeded
- More fresh basil leaves, for garnish

INSTRUCTIONS

1 In a small saucepan over medium-high heat, heat 1 cup water and the sugar until the sugar is fully dissolved.

2 Add in basil and heat 5 minutes longer then remove from the stove and let sit for 30 minutes.

3 Strain the mixture into a pitcher and add the lime juice. Stir until well blended.

4 Serve in glasses over ice with additional basil and lime slices.

YIELDS · 4-6 glasses

ICED RASPBERRY MINT TEA

Karen

This fruity and minty drink won the blue-ribbon rosette in the Cooking with Mint category at the Clinton County 4-H Fair in St Johns, Michigan where we lived when we were raising our kids. This small town is considered the Mint Capital of the United States.

PREP TIME · 15 minutes, plus 30 minutes cooling time

- 1½ cups fresh or frozen raspberries
- 1½ cups extra-fine sugar
- 7 cups water, divided
- 4 peppermint herbal tea bags
- 2 red raspberry herbal tea bags
- Fresh mint leaves and raspberries for garnish (optional)

INSTRUCTIONS

1. Place raspberries in a blender with 3 cups of water. Puree on high for 60 seconds.

2. Strain into the pitcher using a fine colander or a colander lined with cheesecloth, pressing hard on the solids.

3. In a medium saucepan over medium-high heat, stir the remaining 4 cups of water with the sugar until the sugar is completely dissolved.

4. Remove from heat and add in the tea bags. Let cool for 30 minutes.

5. Remove tea bags and pour into the pitcher.

6. Stir well before pouring and serve over ice.

7. Garnish with fresh mint leaves and a few floating fresh raspberries.

YIELDS · 4 servings

SOUL SOOTHER

Rich in electrolytes and vitamin C, our adrenal cocktail drink is especially hydrating and healthier than sports drinks found in our grocery stores today. Remaining hydrated can decrease mood swings, contribute to happier feelings, help improve focus, and reduce anxious and depressive thoughts. Make sure that your main source of hydration is quality H_2O, and if you need something with a little flavor, try a calming adrenal cocktail!

CALMING ADRENAL COCKTAIL

Macey

As a counselor, this is one of my favorite beverages to make when I need electrolytes and other beneficial nutrients which inevitably contribute to more positive mental health. Our physical, mental, and spiritual health are all intertwined, and we are mentally our best whenever we are feeling our best physically and emotionally as well! Bonus—it tastes just like an orange creamsicle!

PREP TIME · 10 minutes

- 8 ounces orange juice
- 2 ounces coconut water
- 2 ounces whole milk
- 1 tablespoon maple syrup
- ¼ teaspoon of salt
- 32-ounce jar with lid

INSTRUCTIONS

1   Mix all ingredients and enjoy! Based on personal preference, you can adjust the ratios of ingredients listed above.

YIELDS · 1 serving

MITCHELL'S MANGO KOMBUCHA

Macey

My husband, Mitchell, is famous for his kombucha making skills. Anyone who knows me knows that I love a good beverage, and his kombucha recipe does not disappoint. It takes patience, but you are well-rewarded at the end of this fermentation process!

PREP TIME · 10-14 days

- 16 cups filtered water, divided
- 12 black tea bags
- 1 gallon container
- 1 cup granulated sugar
- 1 Scoby (a kombucha culture which you can buy on Amazon)
- 1 cup of unflavored kombucha (either bought at the grocery store or reserved from your first batch)
- 1 cheesecloth (to fit the head of your container)
- 1 rubber band
- 20 ounces of fruit juice
- 10 bottling bottles (16 oz.)

Be sure to welcome strangers into your home. By doing this, some people have welcomed angels as guests, without even knowing it.

HEBREW 13:2 (CEV)

INSTRUCTIONS

1 Boil 8 cups of water in a pot on the stove or in a tea kettle.

2 Add your tea bags to the boiling water and let them steep for about 20 minutes.

3 After they have steeped, strain your liquid into a large one-gallon container.

4 Add the sugar to the tea and stir until the sugar is dissolved.

5 Add in the additional 8 cups of water and let the temperature decrease to less than 90 degrees.

6 Add your Scoby to your tea along with 1 cup of unflavored kombucha.

7 Cover your container with cheesecloth and secure it with a rubber band. Place your container in a cool, dark place (we use our closet). The ideal temperature is between 75 to 85 degrees.

8 Let your kombucha sit for 7 to 10 days. This is the first fermentation. You can drink your kombucha now, but we prefer and suggest a second fermentation. Reserve 1 cup of unflavored kombucha for your next batch.

Second Fermentation

1 Pour 2 ounces of fruit juice into a 16-ounce bottling bottle. We prefer tropical juices like mango, pineapple, and peach. (You can also put chunks of fruit in the kombucha and strain before drinking).

2 Fill the rest of the container with kombucha, leaving about one inch or so of space, and seal.

3 Repeat until all of the kombucha has been used.

4 Allow to sit for another 3 to 4 days, opening the bottles occasionally to release carbonation. If you do not open the bottles, the buildup of carbonation can cause them to burst.

5 Transfer to the fridge to stop the carbonation process and enjoy!

YIELDS · 1 gallon

REFRESHING FRESH-SQUEEZED LEMONADE

This recipe was born out of a need to use the abundance of lemons from my Granny Brewer's lemon tree. She sent me home to Michigan with a whole bag full of the best looking lemons I had ever seen. There's nothing I love more on a hot summer day, especially after working hard on the farm, than a cold glass of fresh squeezed lemonade. I make sure to whip up this recipe whenever we have guests, as it is always a refreshing surprise and a nice addition to any lunch recipe. It's a bonus when I get to use my Granny's lemons!

PREP TIME · 20 minutes

COOK TIME · 5 minutes

- 6 cups filtered water, divided
- 1½ cups granulated sugar
- 12 lemons, juiced and seeded
- 8 limes, juiced and seeded
- 2 lemon slices for garnish
- 2 lime slices for garnish

HOSPITALITY HACK

Brew and steep your favorite tea. We personally enjoy chamomile or lemon balm tea. Let cool and then pour into a silicone ice cube mold and put in your freezer. Add these to your drink so that as the tea ice cubes melt, they provide more flavor rather than watering down your drink!

INSTRUCTIONS

1 Combine 1 cup of water and the sugar in a small pot. Heat over medium heat until the sugar is dissolved.

2 Remove from heat and allow to cool.

3 Pour the lemon and lime juice into a pitcher. Add your sugar and water mixture. Add remaining water and stir.

4 Serve over ice and with lemon and lime slices for garnish.

YIELDS · 6-8 servings

ASPARAGUS WRAPS

Karen

This is a simple vegetarian appetizer that tastes so gourmet. I am always asked to share the recipe. And it turns out looking so pretty, too!

PREP TIME · 25 minutes
COOK TIME · 20 minutes

- 1 1/2 cups grated Parmesan cheese
- 8 ounces cream cheese, room temperature
- 15 slices soft white or wheat bread, crusts removed and flattened
- 15 asparagus spears, steamed until very tender (or 15 spears canned)
- 1/2 cup butter, melted

INSTRUCTIONS

1   Preheat the oven to 350 degrees.

2   Line a baking sheet with parchment paper or cooking spray.

3   Mix the cheeses together in a small bowl.

4   Spread mixture evenly over one side of each of the bread slices.

5   Place 1 asparagus spear per piece of bread, laying it diagonally from corner to corner. Bring together the opposite corners and secure them around the spear with a toothpick.

6   Brush each piece of bread well with butter all over, even on the bottom, and place on a baking sheet.

7   Bake at 350 degrees for 20 minutes until lightly browned.

YIELDS · 15 wraps

PAPA'S APPLE BUTTER BARBECUE MEATBALLS

Karen

My father worked for over four decades in the food service industry. He began as a cook in the US Navy before owning his own restaurant in Lansing, Michigan called Pat's Pantry. Over the years, he catered hundreds of parties. He not only served these sweet and tangy appetizer meatballs at such functions, he also made them each year for our family Christmas Eve get together at his house. If you want a shortcut, purchase frozen meatballs, make the sauce, and then place everything in a slow cooker and cook for 4 hours on low.

PREP TIME · 25 minutes

COOK TIME · 25-30 minutes for the meatballs and another 2-4 hours in the slow cooker

Meatballs

- 1 pound ground pork
- 1 pound ground round or ground chuck
- 1 cup dry breadcrumbs
- ½ cup whole or 2% milk
- ¼ cup finely minced onion (or 3 tablespoons dried minced)
- 2 teaspoons Worcestershire sauce
- 2 eggs, lightly beaten
- 1 teaspoon garlic powder
- ¼ teaspoon allspice
- ¼ teaspoon nutmeg
- 1 teaspoon salt
- ½ teaspoon black pepper

Sauce

- 1 bottle (12 oz.) chili sauce (I use Heinz™)
- 1½ cups apple butter
- ¾ cup pure maple syrup
- 1½ tablespoons molasses
- ½ teaspoon garlic powder
- ¼ teaspoon ground cloves
- ½ teaspoon ground cinnamon
- ¼ teaspoon salt

INSTRUCTIONS

1   Preheat the oven to 400 degrees.

2   Mix all meatball ingredients in a large bowl until well blended. Using your hands works best.

3   Divide mixture in three sections. For each of the three sections, form 10 meatballs about 2 inches in diameter, resulting in a total of 30 meatballs.

4   Bake on a large cookie sheet that has been lined with parchment paper or sprayed with cooking spray for 20 to 25 minutes or until no longer pink inside. Watch carefully so they don't burn.

5   Cool slightly if finishing the recipe immediately or cool completely and store in the refrigerator, covered, for up to 3 days or frozen in freezer bags for up to 3 months.

On the day you will serve them

1   In a medium bowl, mix all of the sauce ingredients together.

2   Place meatballs in a slow cooker and pour the sauce over them.

3   Cover and cook on low for 2 to 4 hours and serve.

YIELDS · About 30 meatballs

SPINACH THREE CHEESE DIP

Macey

This is one of my favorite dishes to make, especially on colder days, when I want something warm and filling. It's also fun to make with family and friends and pair with my homemade Sourdough Pretzels *on page 200. Fun fact: the Ehmans are very verbal when it comes to food, and the verdict for this cheese dip was "mmm mmm" from all the Ehman men!*

PREP TIME · 10 minutes

COOK TIME · 40 minutes

- Avocado oil cooking spray
- 1 container (8 oz.) cream cheese, softened
- 1 cup spicy mayonnaise (see *Spicy Mayonnaise* recipe on page 226)
- 1 cup heavy cream
- 2 teaspoons garlic salt
- 1 teaspoon onion powder
- ½ teaspoon black pepper
- 1 package (16 oz.) of baby spinach
- 1 pound bacon, cooked and crumbled
- 1¼ cups shredded pepper jack cheese, divided
- 1¼ cups shredded three cheese blend, divided
- 1 cast iron pan (8-inch)

INSTRUCTIONS

1 Preheat your oven to 350 degrees.

2 Spray the bottom and sides of an 8-inch cast iron pan with avocado oil spray.

3 With a stand mixer, whip cream cheese, mayonnaise, heavy cream, garlic salt, onion powder, and black pepper. Whip until creamy and combined, about 1 to 2 minutes.

4 Mix in your spinach, bacon, and ¾ cup each of the shredded cheeses.

5 Pour the mixture into the cast iron pan. Top with the remaining cheese.

6 Bake for 30 minutes or until bubbly.

7 Turn your oven to low broil and broil until the cheese is a nice golden brown—about 10 minutes.

8 Serve with tortilla chips, crackers, or even pretzels!

YIELDS · 8 servings (or 4 hungry Ehman men)

BLACK-BEAN, MANGO, CORN SALSA

This is a brightly colored south-of-the-border fruit-and-veggie salsa that is a crowd-pleasing favorite any time of the year. Serve with hearty tortilla chips for dipping.

PREP TIME · 20 minutes

- 3 large mangoes, peeled and chopped
- 2 cans (15 oz.) black beans, rinsed and drained
- 2½ cups frozen corn, thawed and drained
- 1 medium red bell pepper chopped
- 1 small red onion, chopped
- 1 medium jalapeno, seeded and minced
- 1 garlic clove, finely minced (or 2 teaspoons store-bought minced garlic)
- ¼ cup chopped cilantro
- 1½ teaspoons salt
- ½ teaspoon pepper
- ⅓ cup lime juice

INSTRUCTIONS

1   Combine all ingredients except for the spices and lime juice, gently tossing them in a large bowl until well incorporated.

2   Sprinkle on the garlic, cilantro, salt, and pepper and drizzle with the lime juice. Toss one more time.

3   Cover and refrigerate until time to serve. This dish is best made about 2 hours before serving.

4   Serve with hearty tortilla chips.

YIELDS · About 8 cups

HAM AND TURKEY PARTY ROLL UPS

Karen

This colorful appetizer was a favorite of many of my kids' friends when they were teenagers. Perfect for a sleepover or for watching a football game. A simple and silly type of party "sushi"! Make sure to get ham and turkey slices of the same size for easier assembly.

PREP TIME · 10 minutes

- 1 tub (8 oz.) veggie or chive and onion cream cheese
- 8 slices uncured deli ham
- 8 slices uncured deli turkey
- 8 sweet or dill pickle spears (we like sweet best), blotted dry with a paper towel
- 32 toothpicks

INSTRUCTIONS

1   Spread the cream cheese evenly over the slices of ham.

2   Top each ham slice with 1 slice of turkey.

3   Place 1 pickle spear on each of the ham/turkey pieces near one edge and roll up tightly.

4   Secure with 4 toothpicks per roll, spaced evenly.

5   Cut each roll into 4 slices so that each slice has a toothpick. Yum!

YIELDS · 32 small "sushi" pieces

MAPLE PEANUT BUTTER PROTEIN BALLS

This recipe was given to us by a dear friend, Mrs. Davis, and tweaked to satisfy my husband's peanut butter and maple syrup addiction! These are great to make ahead and take on family trips. We often pack these in our picnic basket when we go hiking! Don't worry. There's no danger of "leaving a trace behind" with these! They are gobbled up in no time!

PREP TIME · 30 minutes, up to 24 hours

- 5 cups sprouted rolled oats
- ½ cup ground flaxseed
- ½ cup chia seed
- 2 tablespoons sunflower seeds
- 3 cups chunky peanut butter
- 2 cups coconut flakes
- 8 ounces milk chocolate chips
- 1½ cups raw honey
- ½ cup maple syrup

SOUL SOOTHER

Physical activity, specifically outdoors, has been shown to increase feelings of positivity and energy and decrease feelings of stress, anger, and depression. It also has been shown to increase attention span, improve problem-solving skills, and help us to reconnect with ourselves and others. When you are physically active, make sure to stay hydrated and fueled with recipes like this one!

INSTRUCTIONS

1   Mix all of the ingredients above in a large bowl. Use a spoon initially, but eventually, you will need to use your hands to incorporate all ingredients.

2   Roll into one-inch balls. If the mixture is too dry, add equal parts of more peanut butter, honey, and maple syrup.

3   Store in the fridge in an airtight container. Best served if allowed to sit overnight.

YIELDS · 20-30 protein balls (depending on how big you make the protein balls)

HOMEMADE PRETZELS AND CHEESE DIP

Karen

A fun snack to make together with friends or family. You can't beat warm pretzels served straight out of the oven with homemade cheese dip. So good!

PREP TIME · 2 ½ hours, including rise time for the dough

COOK TIME · 20 minutes

Pretzels

- 1 cup very warm, but not boiling, water (105 to 110 degrees)
- 2 tablespoons dry yeast (or 2 packets if using pre-packaged instead of bulk)
- ½ cup + 3 teaspoons honey, divided
- ½ cup butter
- 1 tablespoon salt
- 2½ cups whole milk
- 8 cups bread flour
- Butter for melting and brushing on top
- Coarse salt for topping
- Candy thermometer

INSTRUCTIONS

1 In a large bowl, mix warm water, yeast, and 3 teaspoons of honey. Let the mixture rest.

2 In a large saucepan, melt butter.

3 Add remaining honey, salt, and milk to the melted butter. Heat this to 120 degrees over medium heat (use a candy thermometer).

4 Take off the stove and let cool for 10 minutes, stirring occasionally.

5 Pour milk mixture into yeast mixture and stir well.

6 Fold in flour 2 cups at a time until a slightly stiff dough is formed. You may need to add a little more or less than 8 cups depending on the humidity of the day.

7 Knead dough for 5 to 10 minutes.

8 Place in a large, oiled bowl, cover, and let it rise for 1 to 1½ hours, until doubled in size.

9 Preheat the oven to 350 degrees and lightly spray a cookie sheet with cooking spray.

10 Punch dough down to release air and knead on a lightly floured surface for 5 minutes.

11 Take a piece of dough about the size of a tennis ball. Roll it into a ½-inch thick rope. Make it into a pretzel shape by crossing the ends, leaving about two inches on the ends. Then twist at the intersection of the two ends one time. Fold the ends down to touch the sides, creating a traditional pretzel shape. (You can also just leave them as ropes, if you wish.) Repeat with remaining dough. (Makes 10 to 12 pretzels on average)

12 Place pretzels on the cookie sheet and bake for 20 minutes at 350 degrees until golden brown. Do not over bake.

13 When you remove pretzels from the oven, brush them with additional melted butter, then sprinkle coarse salt on top.

YIELDS · About 10-12 pretzels

Cheese Dip

- 2 tablespoons butter
- 2 tablespoons all-purpose flour
- 1 cup whole milk
- 2 cups extra sharp cheddar cheese, shredded from a block (not bagged)
- ½ teaspoon smoked paprika

INSTRUCTIONS

1 Over medium-low heat, melt the butter in a saucepan.

2 Whisk in flour.

3 Slowly pour in the milk and keep whisking until the mixture thickens slightly.

4 Add in the cheese until it melts.

5 Stir in the paprika.

6 Remove from heat and serve immediately.

YIELDS · About 3 cups

MARSHMALLOW FRUIT DIP

Karen

This creamy dip whips up in a jiffy. Serve it with whole strawberries, pineapple chunks, or kiwi slices. Can also be served with graham crackers too.

PREP TIME · 5 minutes

- 8 ounces cream cheese, room temperature
- 1 jar (7 oz.) of marshmallow fluff
- ½ teaspoon vanilla extract
- ¼ teaspoon almond extract

INSTRUCTIONS

1   Blend all in a small bowl and refrigerate.

2   Remove from the refrigerator 30 minutes before serving.

YIELDS · About 4-6 servings

BREAKFAST &BRUNCH

"When you wake up in the morning, Pooh," said Piglet at last, "what's the first thing you say to yourself?" "What's for breakfast?" said Pooh. "What do you say, Piglet?" "I say, I wonder what's going to happen exciting today?" said Piglet. Pooh nodded thoughtfully. "It's the same thing," he said.

— A.A. MILNE

A great day starts with a fabulous breakfast. Here are some of our favorites to not only serve our families, but to have piping hot and ready in the morning for overnight company as well. Rise and shine! Your homemade breakfast is waiting.

KENZIE & JASON'S SIGNATURE AVOCADO TOAST

Macey

I'm not sure who came up with this recipe so I must credit both my sister-in-law and brother-in-law with this delicious breakfast entree! We took a siblings' trip to Utah in 2021 while I was pregnant with Jasper. Jason and Kenzie made us avocado toast almost every morning of our trip. I have craved their version of avocado toast since then and have become somewhat of an avocado toast snob as a result!

PREP TIME · 10 minutes

COOK TIME · 10 minutes

- 2 slices sourdough bread (see *Sandwich Bread* sourdough recipe on page 198 for a homemade one)
- 1 tablespoon extra-virgin olive oil
- 2 fried eggs, cooked to order
- 4 tablespoons butter, softened and divided
- 2 ounces cream cheese, softened
- ¼ cup guacamole, divided
- 2 ounces feta cheese
- 1 teaspoon everything but the bagel seasoning

INSTRUCTIONS

1   Toast your sourdough bread.

2   While your bread is toasting, heat your olive oil in a small pan such as a cast iron egg skillet.

3   Once your oil is hot, crack your eggs and cook to order.

4   Put your pieces of toast on a plate. Spread 2 tablespoons of butter on each piece of toast.

5   Next, spread 1 ounce of cream cheese on each piece of toast.

6   Next, add a layer of 2 tablespoons of guacamole.

7   Sprinkle each piece of toast with 1 ounce of feta cheese and ½ teaspoon of everything but the bagel seasoning.

8   Add your fried egg on top and enjoy!

YIELDS · 2 pieces of avocado toast

FARMER'S BREAKFAST CASSEROLE

We live on a farm and have laying chickens. In the summertime, that means an abundance of eggs! Frying and scrambling them can become a little boring after a while so this is a creative way to use those eggs! My family loves this dish, and it's a regular feature for our Monday Breakfast-for-Supper nights. We hope you enjoy it as much as we do!

PREP TIME · 30 minutes

COOK TIME · 40 minutes

- 1 tablespoon butter or cooking oil
- 1 medium Vidalia onion, chopped into small pieces
- 1 sweet bell pepper, chopped into small pieces
- 8 ounces of canned mushrooms (or fresh if you prefer and chopped into small pieces)
- 1 pound of your desired meat
- 8 eggs
- 1 cup whole milk or heavy cream
- ½ teaspoon salt
- ¼ teaspoon ground black pepper
- 2 cups of shredded cheese plus some to sprinkle on the top (we prefer mild or sharp cheddar)
- Avocado oil cooking spray
- 1 package (8 oz.) of refrigerated crescent rolls

HOSPITALITY HACK

For perfectly round fried eggs to be used in a breakfast sandwich when having overnight guests, heat a frying pan and melt a tablespoon or two of butter in it. Spray Mason jar rings with cooking spray. Place the rings on the pan and slowly drop 1 cracked egg into each of the rings. Cook for about 5 minutes for a medium yolk. Use tongs to remove the Mason jar rings and serve eggs on biscuits or English muffins along with sausage, bacon, or ham and a slice of cheese.

INSTRUCTIONS

1   Preheat your oven to 375 degrees.

2   In a medium saucepan, add 1 tablespoon of cooking oil or butter and cook your onions, bell pepper, and mushrooms (if using fresh mushrooms), stirring as needed.

3   Once the vegetables are cooked to your desire, set aside in a large bowl.

4   Then, add in your desired meat and cook thoroughly (I use grass fed and grass finished breakfast sausage from our farm).

5   Once your meat is finished cooking, add it to the large bowl of vegetables.

6   While your vegetables and meat are cooking, whisk 8 eggs in a large bowl.

7   Add in and whisk your milk, salt, and pepper into the egg mixture.

8   Add 2 cups of cheese to your egg mixture as well.

9   Spray your 9 x 13-inch baking dish with avocado oil.

10 Open your crescent roll package and spread the crescent rolls across the entirety of the bottom of the baking dish, making sure to pinch the seams together.

11 Add your vegetables and meat to your baking dish.

12 Pour your egg mixture over the top of your vegetables and meat.

13 Cover the top of the dish with your desired cheese.

14 Bake uncovered for 40 minutes.

15 Let sit for 5 minutes before digging in!

YIELDS · 10 generous sized portions or 15 smaller portions

VEGGIE STRATA

Karen

This veggie-laden dish is a hearty offering that works well for feeding a brunch crowd. If you would rather make a meat version, substitute 1 pound of browned and drained pork or turkey sausage for the diced peppers and broccoli.

PREP TIME · 10 minutes
COOK TIME · 60-75 minutes

- ½ cup diced green pepper
- ½ cup diced red pepper
- ½ cup diced onion
- 2 tablespoons olive oil
- 1 can (6 oz.) of tomatoes with green chilies, undrained
- 9 large eggs
- ¾ cup all-purpose flour
- 2 teaspooons baking powder
- ½ teaspoon salt

- 1 teaspoon chopped fresh garlic (or ½ teaspoon dried minced garlic)
- 1½ cups frozen corn, thawed
- 12 ounces sour cream
- 12 ounces cottage cheese
- 1 cup frozen broccoli florets, thawed, drained, and coarsely chopped
- 1½ cups sharp cheddar cheese
- 1 cup shredded Gruyère cheese
- ½ cup Romano cheese

INSTRUCTIONS

1   In a skillet, lightly sauté peppers and onion in olive oil for 3 to 5 minutes.

2   Stir in tomatoes and set aside.

3   In a large bowl, beat eggs well and then stir in flour, baking powder, salt, garlic, corn, sour cream, and cottage cheese, mixing well.

4   Gently fold in the broccoli and the rest of the cheeses.

5   Stir in the tomato mixture.

6   Pour into a greased 9 x 13-inch pan and bake at 350 degrees for 60 to 75 minutes until puffed and golden.

YIELDS · 12 servings

OVERNIGHT FRENCH TOAST

Karen

This is a fabulous make-ahead way to have a scrumptious breakfast ready in the morning. Perfect for a busy Sunday when you are getting everyone ready for church. The recipe calls for sourdough or French bread, but you can use whole-grain, raisin bread, or almost anything.

PREP TIME · 15 minutes

COOK TIME · 40-50 minutes (but sits overnight at least 8 hours before baking)

French Toast

- ½ cup unsalted butter
- 1 cup brown sugar
- Cooking spray
- 1 loaf (8 oz.) crusty sourdough or French bread, cut into bite-sized pieces
- 2 cups whole milk
- 6 large eggs, lightly beaten
- ¼ cup sugar
- 1 teaspoon each of vanilla and orange extract (or 2 teaspoons vanilla extract)
- ⅔ cup raisins or dried cherries or cranberries, (optional)

Topping

- 3 tablespoons brown sugar
- ¾ teaspoon ground cinnamon
- ¼ teaspoon ground nutmeg

INSTRUCTIONS

1   The night before serving, melt butter in a small saucepan over low heat.

2   Stir in brown sugar until dissolved.

3   Pour butter-brown sugar mixture into a 9 x 13-inch pan that has been buttered or sprayed with cooking spray.

4   Place bread pieces evenly in the pan.

5   In a bowl, whisk milk, eggs, sugar, extracts, and raisins together and pour over bread.

6   Press bread down with a large spoon so it is saturated with the liquid.

7   Cover with plastic wrap and chill for at least 8 hours or overnight.

8   When ready to bake, mix remaining brown sugar, cinnamon, and nutmeg and sprinkle over the top.

9   Bake, uncovered, in a 350-degree oven for 40 to 50 minutes or until lightly browned.

10 To serve, sprinkle with powdered sugar or drizzle with pure maple syrup.

YIELDS · 8 servings

EASY OVERNIGHT SOAKED PANCAKES

Macey

One of my favorite childhood memories is waking up at my grandparents' house on Saturday mornings to a smorgasbord of breakfast foods cooked by my Mema. Pancakes were always included, and I finally created a recipe that tastes exactly like the pancakes of my childhood. This recipe has the added bonus of being more easily digestible, and thus, better for our gut health. Every time I take a bite of these soaked pancakes, I'm transported back in time, honoring my Mema's memory as I continue this tradition with my husband and son.

PREP TIME · 8-12 hours

COOK TIME · About 5 minutes per pan of pancakes

- 2 cups milk (we use raw milk from a local farmer—thanks Martin family!)
- 2 cups flour
- 2 eggs
- ½ teaspoon salt
- 1 teaspoon baking soda
- 2 tablespoons butter, melted
- 1 stick butter, softened for cooking and topping

INSTRUCTIONS

1. Whisk your milk and flour together, cover, and let sit overnight. In the morning, you should see "bubbles" across the surface of your mixture.

2. Stir in your eggs, salt, baking soda, and melted butter.

3. Heat your medium pan over medium heat and melt 1 tablespoon of butter.

4. Once the pan is hot, scoop ⅓ cup of batter in a measuring cup and pour into the pan.

5. Once you see bubbles forming, flip your pancake.

6. Cook for about 2 minutes more or until golden brown, take your pancake out of the pan, and repeat the process starting with 1 tablespoon of butter.

7. Serve with your favorite toppings. We love to top our pancakes with more butter, maple syrup, peanut butter, and fresh fruit! To make this a truly Southern meal, make sure to add scrambled eggs and bacon (and maybe some sausage patties and toast with jam)! What can I say, Southerners like to eat!

YIELDS · 10 pancakes

SPICED APPLE SLOW COOKER OATMEAL

Karen

This warm and creamy comfort food will be piping hot and waiting for you in the morning after having simmered in your slow cooker all night. You can even modify the recipe by adding other fruits you like such as diced peaches, dried cranberries, or chopped pears. Stir in walnuts, pecans, or even peanut butter in the morning. So simple and so scrumptious!

PREP TIME · 5 minutes

COOK TIME · 7 hours

- Cooking spray
- 2 cups peeled, cubed, tart cooking apples (Granny Smith, Spy, or Golden Delicious)
- 1½ cup uncooked steel-cut oats (do **NOT** use old-fashioned, quick, or instant oats)
- 3 cups whole or 2% milk
- 2½ cups water
- 1½ teaspoon cinnamon
- ½ teaspoon ground nutmeg
- ¼ cup brown sugar
- ¼ cup maple syrup
- 3 tablespoons butter, cut into small pieces
- 1 teaspoon vanilla
- ¼ teaspoon salt

> ## SOUL SOOTHER
>
> Our families have tried to be more intentional with taking a Sabbath and resting one day a week. God tells us in His Word to rest and that it is for our good to rest. Science reiterates this by showing that resting decreases anxiety, worry and stress and increases self-awareness, self-care, enriching relationships, spirituality, and being better able to enjoy the results of our work which leads to producing even better results after our time of rest. Recipes like this one enable us to take and enjoy a Sabbath. We can make everything the night before and wake up to an already cooked meal to enjoy with family!

INSTRUCTIONS

1. Butter the inside of a 4 or 6 quart slow cooker or spray it with cooking spray.

2. Add all the ingredients, stirring well.

3. Cover and cook on low for 6 to 7 hours.

4. Serve with pure maple syrup and additional butter, if desired.

YIELDS · 8 servings

BROWN SUGAR BACON

Karen

When our sons were teenagers, I could not make enough of this brown sugar bacon on Saturday mornings when their friends had all spent the night the evening before. It turns out perfectly crisp, with a balanced combination of salty and sweet.

PREP TIME · 5 minutes
COOK TIME · 18-20 minutes

- ½ cup brown sugar
- 3 tablespoons Dijon mustard
- Freshly ground black pepper
- 1 pound of thick cut bacon

INSTRUCTIONS

1   Preheat the oven to 400 degrees.

2   In a small bowl combine brown sugar and mustard.

3   Line a baking sheet with foil or parchment paper.

4   Place a metal cooling rack on the lined baking sheet.

5   Put bacon on the rack and use a pastry brush to coat the bacon strips with the brown sugar mixture.

6   Sparsely sprinkle with pepper.

7   Bake for 18 to 20 minutes until crispy and browned.

YIELDS · 6-8 servings

Let me experience your faithful love in the morning, for I trust in you. Reveal to me
the way I should go because I appeal to you.

PSALM 143:8 (CSB)

MITCHELL'S SOAKED OATMEAL PANCAKES

Macey

My husband, Mitchell, is a fan of the popular podcaster Ben Greenfield. Through him, he found this recipe for soaked oatmeal pancakes. They remind him of the pancakes he ate as a child at a local restaurant in mid-Michigan, and we knew we had to recreate them with an Ehman flair (aka walnuts and cinnamon)! He smothers these pancakes with peanut butter and fresh fruit, and they are a regular feature in our kitchen!

PREP TIME · 32 hours

COOK TIME · About 5 minutes per pan of pancakes

- 3 cups sprouted rolled oats
- ½ a lemon, juiced (or 1 tablespoon whey)
- 4 eggs
- 4 tablespoons butter
- 2 teaspoons baking soda
- 1 tablespoon vanilla
- ½ cup crushed walnuts (optional)
- 1 teaspoon cinnamon (optional)

INSTRUCTIONS

1. Rinse sprouted rolled oats four to five times in filtered water using a colander.

2. In a covered bowl, soak your oats in filtered water overnight.

3. In the morning, rinse the oats again in a colander.

4. Put the oats back in the bowl and add 1 tablespoon of whey or the juice from ½ a lemon.

5. Cover again for 24 hours.

6. Rinse one last time in a colander, and your oats are ready to use. This is a long process but worth it because it makes the oats easily digestible!

7. In the bowl of oats, add 4 eggs, 4 tablespoons of butter, 2 teaspoons of baking soda, 1 tablespoon of vanilla, ½ cup of crushed walnuts, and 1 teaspoon of cinnamon. Whisk until combined.

8. Heat your medium pan and melt 1 tablespoon of butter.

9. Once the pan is hot, scoop ⅓ cup of batter in a measuring cup and pour into the pan.

10. Once you see "bubbles" forming, flip your pancake.

11. Cook for about 2 minutes more or until golden brown, take your pancake out of the pan, and repeat starting with 1 tablespoon of butter.

YIELDS · 8-10 pancakes

FETA AND SPINACH QUICHE

Karen

This is so easy to assemble and cook if you use a store-bought crust. Or, if you prefer homemade, use the recipe from Cheesy Chicken Pot Pie *on page 104. Either way, it is a flavorful start to any day. If you want to add meat, toss in about a ½ cup cooked, crumbled bacon and reduce the spinach down to ½ a cup.*

PREP TIME · 10 minutes
COOK TIME · 30 minutes

- 1 frozen or refrigerated pie crust
- 3 tablespoons chopped onions
- 1¼ cups chopped fresh spinach
- ⅓ cup feta cheese crumbles
- ½ cup extra-sharp shredded cheddar cheese
- 5 large or 6 medium eggs

- 1 teaspoon garlic powder
- ¾ teaspoon salt
- ½ teaspoon pepper
- 2 dashes Tabasco™ sauce
- 1 tablespoon cold butter, cut into six pieces

- INSTRUCTIONS

1 Preheat the oven to 350 degrees.

2 *If pie crust is frozen:* thaw and prick all over the bottom with a fork and pre-bake for 10 minutes.

 If using a refrigerated or homemade crust: roll out and place in the pan, crimping the edges. Prick the bottom all over with a fork and bake for 10 minutes.

3 Remove from the oven. Cool slightly and place on a cookie sheet.

4 In a medium bowl, combine onion, spinach, feta, and cheddar cheese and spoon into the crust.

5 In a large bowl, whisk together the eggs, garlic powder, salt, pepper, and Tabasco.

6 Carefully pour the egg mixture into the crust and then dot with the pieces of the butter, evenly spaced.

7 Bake at 350 for 25 to 30 minutes until completely set.

YIELDS · 6 servings

LOADED SOUTHWEST BREAKFAST BAKED POTATOES *Macey*

This recipe was one that I pieced together when our fridge was low and we needed to go to the grocery store. Those kinds of recipes always seem to be the best, and this is now a go to recipe in our house! Baked salmon is also a surprisingly good topping for this dish!

PREP TIME · 10 minutes
COOK TIME · 45 minutes

- 2 large Yukon gold potatoes
- Avocado oil cooking spray
- 3 tablespoons butter, divided
- Salt, to taste
- 2 cloves garlic, minced
- 1 bell pepper, chopped
- 8 ounces fresh mushrooms, chopped
- 1 Vidalia onion, chopped
- 4 eggs
- 1 tablespoon milk
- Feta cheese, for topping
- Sour cream, for topping
- Salsa, for topping
- Favorite hot sauce, for topping

INSTRUCTIONS

1. Preheat your oven to 400 degrees.

2. Wash your potatoes and pierce them multiple times with a fork.

3. Spray each potato with avocado oil and salt each potato with salt.

4. Bake your potatoes for 45 minutes or until done.

5. About 15 minutes before the potatoes are done cooking, prepare your egg and vegetable scramble.

6. Melt 1 tablespoon of butter in a nonstick pan over medium heat.

7. Add your garlic and vegetables to the pan and cook until they are soft and the garlic is fragrant, about 15 minutes.

8. Add 4 eggs and 1 tablespoon of milk to the vegetable mixture and scramble.

9. Take your potatoes out of your oven and slice open each potato.

10. Put 1 tablespoon of butter on each potato.

11. Top with scrambled egg and vegetable mixture, feta cheese, sour cream, salsa, and a few drops of hot sauce.

12. Serve and enjoy!

YIELDS · 2 baked potatoes

SIMPLE STOVETOP JAM

Macey

We love this simple jam recipe, especially because it only contains three ingredients, all of which I can pronounce! You can use any fruit, but our favorites are fresh picked strawberries and blueberries from our farm orchard!

PREP TIME · 5 minutes
COOK TIME · 15 minutes

- 2 cups of your favorite fruit
- 1 tablespoon butter
- 1 tablespoon maple syrup

INSTRUCTIONS

1   Cut your fruit into small to medium pieces.

2   Put butter or olive oil in a nonstick pan.

3   Allow the butter to melt, and then put your fruit and maple syrup in the pan.

4   Stir until all of the fruit is cooked, about 15 minutes.

5   Take your spatula and mash the fruit to your desired consistency.

6   Continue cooking until desired thickness is reached.

7   Store in the fridge and consume within 3 to 5 days.

YIELDS · 1 cup

PRESSURE COOKER YOGURT

This recipe is one that I tweaked from a dear friend and mentor in Michigan, Maggie. We love making our own yogurt, and this recipe is such a simple one! All it takes is a little time and patience.

PREP TIME · 15 minutes

COOK TIME · 24 hours

- 1 cup yogurt culture
- 56 ounces whole milk (we use raw milk from a local farmer—thanks Martin family!)
- 2 containers (32 oz.) with lids
- Warm tap water (enough to fill to max line of pressure cooker)
- Pressure cooker

INSTRUCTIONS

1. In each 32-ounce container, add ½ cup yogurt (This is your starter culture. I used organic yogurt from the grocery store for my very first batch).

2. Fill each jar with your whole milk all the way to just below the threads of the jar, put the lids on, and shake until the yogurt is incorporated throughout.

3. Put the jars in your pressure cooker and fill the pot with warm tap water up to the shoulders of each jar (even if that is above the max line for your pressure cooker).

4. Push the Yogurt button until you see the option for a 24-hour culture.

5. When the cycle ends, remove and wipe down the jars and refrigerate until cold.

6. Enjoy as a yogurt parfait (see *Maple Yogurt Parfaits* on page 52 for inspiration) or as the base for a yummy smoothie!

YIELDS · 64 ounces

MAPLE YOGURT PARFAITS

Macey

This is my family's favorite quick, go-to breakfast when we're in a hurry, especially on Sunday mornings since our service starts at 9:30! I love this breakfast option because we can each customize our own parfait depending on personal preferences. I usually set out all of the options and allow everyone to build their own yogurt parfait!

PREP TIME · 15 minutes

- ⅓ cup yogurt (see *Pressure Cooker Yogurt* recipe on page 51 if you desire to make your own)
- 1 tablespoon maple syrup
- 2 tablespoons chocolate chips
- ¼ cup of your favorite granola
- ¼ cup of your favorite fruit
- 1 teaspoon chia and/or hemp seeds
- Other favorite toppings

INSTRUCTIONS

1   Put yogurt in your bowl.

2   Drizzle maple syrup into your bowl. Exclude the maple syrup if you use an already flavored or sweetened yogurt. Stir to combine.

3   Add in your favorite toppings. For my family, we like to include chocolate chips, our favorite brand of granola (my favorite is pumpkin flavored, my husband's favorite is vanilla flavored), as well as fresh blueberries from our front yard and strawberries from the farmer's market. We also enjoy bananas and mangoes in our yogurt parfaits. You can add 1 teaspoon of chia seeds and/or hemp seeds for extra nutrients as well!

YIELDS · 1 bowl

SOUPS & SALADS

"A home is a place where a pot of fresh soup simmers gently on the hob, filling the kitchen with soft aromas and filling your heart, and later your tummy, with joy."

— CHEF KEITH FLOYD

Sometimes offering a simple meal of a soup combined with a refreshing salad is just the right call for lunch or a light dinner. With the recipes in this section, you can offer a variety of savory soups and snappy salads to nourish your family, friends, and other guests.

MISS DEANN'S SEAFOOD CHOWDER

 Macey

My mama's seafood chowder is what we all request for holidays and special occasions because it is just that good. When I moved from Georgia to Michigan, I knew that I needed to recreate this beloved recipe, a taste of home when I was so far away from where I grew up. If you're ever in my mama's neck of the woods, make sure to ask her for a bowl! Like any Southern belle, she'll definitely oblige!

PREP TIME · 30 minutes
COOK TIME · 1 hour

- ½ pint heavy cream
- 2 teaspoons Cajun seasoning, divided
- ½ pound Yukon gold potatoes, cut into small chunks
- ½ pound crab meat, cut into small chunks
- ½ pound shrimp, cut into small chunks
- 1 tablespoon butter
- ½ cup whole milk
- 2 tablespoons cornstarch
- 1 bottle (8 oz.) of clam juice

INSTRUCTIONS

1 Pour the heavy cream in a large pot on low to medium heat.

2 Put 1 teaspoon of Cajun seasoning in with the heavy cream and stir occasionally.

3 Boil potatoes in a pot of water until done (about 20 minutes).

4 Drain your potatoes and then pour into the pot with heavy cream.

5 Season your seafood with the rest of the Cajun seasoning.

6 Sauté the shrimp and crab in 1 tablespoon butter in a medium pan until cooked (about 5 to 10 minutes).

7 Put cooked meat in the pot with the heavy cream and potatoes.

8 Pour ¼ cup of the milk into a saucepan along with the cornstarch. Stir with a whisk constantly.

9 As it thickens, add the rest of the milk.

10 When it thickens, pour in your clam juice. Stir to incorporate.

11 Then, pour into your pot.

12 Allow to simmer on low stirring occasionally for at least 30 minutes—the longer the better!

13 Enjoy with your favorite crackers or bread!

YIELDS · 8-10 servings

CHICKEN WILD RICE SOUP

Karen

My copy-cat version of a soup my daughter, Kenna, loved as a child at Panera Bread. I invented it for her 12th birthday dinner. For fun, purchase bread bowls for serving. The soup is thick enough to keep the bread from getting soggy.

PREP TIME · 20 minutes

COOK TIME · 45-60 minutes

- ½ cup butter
- 1 medium onion, finely chopped
- 1 cup chopped, peeled carrots
- ½ cup celery, finely minced
- ¾ cup all-purpose flour
- 6 cups chicken stock (or 6 cups water with bouillon cubes or chicken base paste to taste)
- 1 package (6 oz.) long grain and wild rice
- 2 cups chopped, cooked chicken
- 3 tablespoons cooking sherry (optional)

INSTRUCTIONS

1 In a large soup pot, melt butter and sauté onions, carrots, and celery until tender over medium heat, about 10 minutes.

2 Slowly whisk in flour.

3 Gradually add stock until mixture comes to a boil, stirring constantly.

4 Reduce heat to medium-low and let simmer while you make the rice, stirring occasionally.

5 Prepare rice as directed on the box, omitting oil and salt.

6 Add rice and chicken to soup and simmer for 10 minutes, stirring occasionally. Add more water if it gets too thick.

7 Add sherry.

8 Serve with a loaf of hearty bread.

YIELDS · 8-10 servings

HEARTY SPLIT PEA SOUP

Karen

I have been making this recipe since the first year I was married. My Grandpa Bob used to always put a splash of apple cider vinegar in his split pea soup, so that is how I serve it. I also sprinkle some grated Parmesan on top. To make a vegetarian version, omit the ham and use vegetable broth instead of chicken broth.

PREP TIME · 15 minutes
COOK TIME · 2 hours 15 minutes

- 2 cups dried split peas
- ¼ cup barley
- ½ cup dried lima beans
- 9 cups chicken stock (or equivalent water mixed with bouillon or stock paste)
- 2 medium onions, chopped
- 3 bay leaves
- 1 teaspoon dried basil
- 1 teaspoon dried thyme
- ½ teaspoon salt
- 2 large carrots, peeled and sliced
- 1 large red potato, peeled and cut into small chunks
- 2 celery stalks, finely minced
- 2 cups chopped, cooked ham
- Apple cider vinegar, croutons, and fresh Parmesan cheese for garnish

INSTRUCTIONS

1 Place the peas, barley, and lima beans, and stock in a large soup pot with the onions and all seasonings.

2 Cook, uncovered, over low heat for about 1½ hours, stirring occasionally.

3 Add the remaining vegetables and ham and continue cooking, uncovered, for about 30-45 minutes until the vegetables are tender.

4 If the soup gets too thick, you may add a little more water.

5 Serve each bowl with a tiny dash of apple cider vinegar, some freshly grated Parmesan cheese on top, and sprinkled with a few croutons.

YIELDS · 8 servings

PAPA PAT'S NAVY BEAN SOUP

Karen

My father was one of eight children who was raised in Kentucky by his preacher daddy and homemaker mama. Only one of his siblings—my Aunt Susie—is still living. Aunt Susie is well into her eighties and she still remembers her mama, my Grandma Truly Patterson, making navy bean soup with ham when she was little. My dad remembered it too and he taught me how to make it. It was something he served in his restaurant, Pat's Pantry. I never knew my grandma because she was killed in a car-train accident over a decade before I was born, but I'm told she was a kind and gentle woman who faithfully served Jesus and who loved reading her old black leather Bible—which I now own. I think about her whenever this hearty soup is simmering on my stove and I can't wait to meet her in heaven someday.

PREP TIME · 15 minutes, plus 8 hours soak time for the beans
COOK TIME · 1 hour 45 minutes

- 1 pound dried navy beans
- 3 tablespoons butter
- 2 medium yellow onions, chopped
- 2 celery ribs, chopped
- 2 medium carrots, chopped
- 2 cloves minced garlic (or 1½ teaspoons dried)
- 8 cups chicken broth
- 3 bay leaves
- 1 teaspoon dried thyme
- 1 teaspoon dried parsley
- 1 teaspoon pepper
- ½ teaspoon salt
- 2 cups cubed fully cooked ham

INSTRUCTIONS

1 Place beans in a large kettle and add water to cover by about 3 inches.

2 Soak for 8 hours or overnight. Drain.

3 In a large kettle, heat butter over medium heat and sauté onion, celery, and carrots in the garlic for 5 minutes.

4 Add in drained beans, chicken broth, remaining spices, and ham.

5 Bring to a low boil over medium-high heat and immediately turn heat to the lowest setting.

6 Cover and simmer for 1 hour, stirring occasionally.

7 Remove cover and simmer 30-45 minutes longer, uncovered, or until beans are tender and soup thickens.

8 Discard bay leaves and serve.

YIELDS · 8 servings

CHEESY CORN CHOWDER

Karen

This is our family's favorite from-scratch soup. Loaded with Yukon Gold potatoes, crisp corn kernels, and crumbled bacon (or diced ham). When I make it my kids—and all their friends—come running. Serve with a crusty, whole-grain bread.

PREP TIME · 20 minutes

COOK TIME · 60-75 minutes

- 4 cups chicken stock (or 4 cups water with bouillon paste or cubes to taste)
- 4 cups chopped, peeled Yukon Gold potatoes
- ½ cup finely chopped celery
- 1 medium minced onion
- 3 tablespoons butter
- 2 cups cooked, crumbled bacon or chopped cooked ham (I use Al Fresco™ fully cooked uncured chicken bacon)
- 1½ cups corn kernels (leftover corn on the cob is great for this!)
- 1 can (14.75 oz.) cream style corn
- 2 cans (10.5 oz.) cream of chicken soup
- 1½ cups extra-sharp cheddar cheese
- 8 ounces sour cream
- Salt and pepper, to taste

SOUL SOOTHER

Karen mentioned that her kids and kids' friends come running to the dinner table when she makes her corn chowder. There are mental health benefits to eating together as a family and with friends. Specifically, it increases self-esteem and resilience and protects against anxiety and depression in children and adults. Keep having those family meals! It's worth it!

INSTRUCTIONS

1. In a large soup pot, combine the stock, potatoes, celery, and onions.

2. Cook over medium heat, covered, for 30 minutes or until potatoes are tender, adding a little water if necessary.

3. Then add butter, bacon, corn, cream style corn, cream of chicken soup, and cheddar cheese.

4. Reduce heat to low and simmer, uncovered for about 45 minutes, stirring occasionally.

5. Stir in sour cream, salt, and pepper until well blended.

6. Simmer for 5 more minutes and serve.

YIELDS · 8-10 servings

IRISH POTATO SOUP

Macey

It's a cold, dreary day as I write this section, and what better to write about than a warm, yummy soup! My husband loves this recipe because it's hearty and filling, and I love it because it reminds me of my mom's loaded baked potato soup. Excuse me while I head to my kitchen—a bowl of warmth and home, coming right up!

PREP TIME · 1 hour

COOK TIME · 30 minutes or as long as desired

- 1 pound bacon, cooked and chopped
- 2 pounds Yukon gold potatoes, washed and diced
- 1 onion, diced
- 1 stalk celery, diced
- 3 tablespoons garlic, minced
- 2½ cups bone broth
- 1 teaspoon salt
- 1 teaspoon pepper
- 1 tablespoon dried parsley
- 4 tablespoons butter
- ⅓ cup flour
- 3 cups whole milk
- 2 cups sharp cheddar cheese plus desired amount for serving
- ½ cup sour cream

INSTRUCTIONS

1   Take a ½ pound of your cooked bacon and put it in your fridge for serving.

2   Take the other ½ pound and put it in a large pot.

3   Boil your potatoes in a pot of water for 20 to 25 minutes until fork tender.

4   Drain and add to your large pot with the bacon.

5   While your potatoes are cooking, sauté your diced onion, celery, and garlic until the onion is translucent.

6   Add all of these ingredients to your large pot.

7   Turn your large pot on medium heat. Add in broth, salt, pepper, and parsley.

8   In your saucepan, melt the butter. (If you use the same pan that you cooked your onion, celery, and garlic, you will get a very nice flavor).

9   Add in your flour and whisk for 1 minute.

10   Slowly add in your milk (¼ cup at a time) and whisk constantly. Continue until your mixture thickens, about 5 to 10 minutes.

11   Add in your cheese and sour cream, and turn your soup down to simmer on low, stirring occasionally. The longer it simmers, the better!

12   Serve hot with my sourdough *Irish Soda Bread* recipe on page 196 or your favorite crackers!

YIELDS · 8-10 servings

Share with the Lord's people who are in need. Practice hospitality.

ROMANS 12:13

HEARTY ITALIAN SAUSAGE & RICE SLOW COOKER SOUP

Macey

This is my adaptation of the beloved Zuppa Toscana soup. My family loves a hearty soup, and this one does not disappoint. I developed this recipe while in graduate school when on a tight budget and eating out wasn't always an option. Aren't the best recipes made this way—a recipe tweak with whatever you have in your fridge? My husband says it's one of his all-time favorites, and as he was a former chef, that's a true compliment! This is a recipe that you'll definitely want to make for your company!

PREP TIME · 30 minutes

COOK TIME · 8 hours

- 4 cups bone broth
- 1 pound bacon, cooked and chopped
- 1 pound ground spicy Italian sausage, browned
- ½ pound Yukon gold potatoes, diced
- 1 medium Vidalia onion, diced
- 2 tablespoons garlic, minced
- 1 tablespoon butter
- 2 tablespoons flour
- 1 cup heavy cream
- 1 to 2 cups rice (depending on preference)
- 1 teaspoon salt
- 1 teaspoon pepper
- ½ teaspoon red pepper flakes
- 16 ounces kale, destemmed

INSTRUCTIONS

1   Before you begin, pour your bone broth into your slow cooker and put it on the lowest setting. I usually set mine to cook for 8 hours.

2   Add your bacon, ground sausage, and potatoes into your slow cooker.

3   Cook your diced onion and minced garlic in a saucepan with 1 tablespoon butter until the onion is translucent.

4   Add your onions and garlic to your slow cooker.

5   In the same saucepan, add your heavy cream and 1 tablespoon of flour at a time, whisking vigorously and constantly until combined and mixture thickens.

6   Add to your slow cooker.

7   Next, add 1 to 2 cups of rice to your slow cooker depending on preference. (If you desire it to be a more soup-like consistency, use 1 cup of rice or less).

8   Add salt, pepper, and red pepper flakes to your soup.

9   Allow to cook on low for 6 to 8 hours, stirring occasionally.

10   With 1 hour left, add 16 ounces of kale and stir to incorporate.

YIELDS · 8-10 servings

MOM'S MIDWEST TURKEY-PUMPKIN CHILI

A new veggie twist on a meaty classic favorite. Rustle up a pot of it on an extra "chilly" day. Get it? Serve with one of our cornbread recipes or our sourdough biscuits.

PREP TIME · 20 minutes

COOK TIME · 55 minutes

- 1 medium onion, chopped
- 2 cloves garlic minced (or 2 teaspoons minced fresh)
- 1 pound lean ground turkey
- 1 medium green bell pepper, chopped
- 2 tablespoons olive oil
- 1 can (14 oz.) petite diced tomatoes with juices
- 1½ cups canned pumpkin
- 1 can (8 oz.) tomato sauce
- 2 cans (14 oz.) red beans, drained
- 2½ tablespoons chili powder
- 1 teaspoon smoked paprika
- ½ teaspoon ground cumin
- ½ teaspoon dried oregano
- 3 cups chicken broth
- 3 to 4 dashes of tabasco sauce
- 1 tablespoon brown sugar
- ½ teaspoon salt
- ¼ teaspoon pepper

INSTRUCTIONS

1. In a large soup pot over medium-high heat, sauté onion, garlic, turkey, and green pepper in the olive oil until turkey is browned, about 10 minutes.

2. Add the rest of the ingredients and turn heat down to low.

3. Simmer uncovered for 45 minutes, stirring occasionally.

4. If it seems too thick, add a little water.

YIELDS · 6-8 servings

TOMATO HERB SOUP

Karen

My friend Janee is the soup queen. She makes the most mouth-watering and unique varieties, including this one. I serve this with grilled cheeses made with sourdough bread and using sharp cheddar, Gruyère, and Swiss. The perfect comfort food combination.

PREP TIME · 15 minutes

COOK TIME · 45 minutes roasting the tomatoes, plus 45 minutes simmering the soup

- 3 pounds Roma tomatoes, cored
- ¼ cup, plus 2 tablespoons olive oil, divided
- 1 tablespoon salt
- 1½ teaspoons black pepper
- 2 cups chopped onion
- 6 cloves fresh garlic, minced (about 1½ tablespoons)
- 4 tablespoons butter
- 1 teaspoon dried thyme
- 4 cups chicken stock (or equivalent water mixed with bouillon or stock paste)
- 1 can (28 oz.) petite diced tomatoes
- 4 cups fresh basil, finely chopped
- Immersion blender or traditional blender

INSTRUCTIONS

1   Preheat the oven to 400 degrees.

2   Line a large cooking sheet with edges with parchment paper or spray with cooking spray.

3   Place the Roma tomatoes in a large bowl, and drizzle them with ¼ cup olive oil, salt, and pepper. Toss well.

4   Spread tomatoes out on the pan and roast for 45 minutes.

5   While the tomatoes are roasting, sauté the onions and garlic in the 2 tablespoons olive oil and the butter in a large stock pot.

6   Add the rest of the ingredients and simmer uncovered over medium low heat for 40 minutes, stirring occasionally.

7   Once the tomatoes are done roasting in the oven, cool slightly and add them to the stock pot.

8   Using an immersion blender, puree the soup. If you don't own an immersion blender, you may puree the soup in a traditional blender, working in batches and adding it back into the pot.

9   Simmer for 5 more minutes and serve.

YIELDS · 6-8 servings

NOURISHING VEGETABLE SOUP

This recipe was made with lots of love when my husband was sick. I was looking for a recipe that would nourish his body and nurse him back to health. It's one I make when any of my loved ones are under the weather. What we put into our bodies is so important for health and wellness and for us to function optimally, and this recipe was created with that in mind. I've also found that when our physical selves are healthy, our mental and emotional selves are as well! This soup truly nourishes the mind, body, and soul!

PREP TIME · 15 minutes
COOK TIME · 45 minutes

- 2 cups bone broth
- 2 cups whole milk
- ½ cup white rice
- 3 large carrots, chopped
- 8 ounces of broccoli, chopped
- 1 medium bell pepper, chopped
- 1 medium zucchini, chopped
- 1 can (15 oz.) full fat coconut milk
- 1 tablespoon ground ginger
- 1 teaspoon ground turmeric
- 2 tablespoons lime juice
- 2 tablespoons coconut aminos
- ½ teaspoon salt

INSTRUCTIONS

1   Place all ingredients in a pot, cover, and bring to a boil.

2   Reduce the heat and simmer on low for about 45 minutes or until your vegetables are cooked as desired.

3   This is a recipe where I use the vegetables listed above (if I have them on hand) and/or any other vegetables that are in my fridge or pantry.

4   I also add 1 pound of cooked meat like sausage, ground beef, or ground venison for an even heartier meal.

YIELDS · 8-10 servings

WHITE CHICKEN CHILI

Macey

This is a recipe from a dear friend, Kali. She's a mentor of sorts to me when it comes to fueling my body with nutrient dense foods. She's taught me that eating ancestrally can still be fun, exciting, and delicious! So, this is my spin on an already scrumptious meal—perfect for crisp autumn and winter days!

PREP TIME · 30 minutes

COOK TIME · 1 ½ hours

- 2½ pounds of chicken breasts
- 1 teaspoon salt
- ½ teaspoon black pepper
- 1 teaspoon cumin
- 1 teaspoon oregano
- ½ teaspoon chili powder
- 2 tablespoons butter
- 1 jalapeno, diced
- 1 medium Vidalia onion, diced

- 2 tablespoons garlic, minced
- ¼ teaspoon cayenne pepper
- 2 cans (15 oz.) beans (Great Northern white beans or navy beans work well)
- 1 bag (15 oz.) of sweet yellow corn
- 3 cups bone broth
- 1 cup heavy cream
- Avocado oil spray

INSTRUCTIONS

1. Preheat your oven to 400 degrees.
2. Line a baking sheet with parchment paper.
3. Arrange your chicken breasts on the baking sheet.
4. Spray them lightly with avocado oil spray, and season with salt, black pepper, cumin, oregano, chili powder, and cayenne pepper.
5. Bake for 20 to 25 minutes or until cooked thoroughly.
6. Melt your butter in a large pot.
7. Add in your jalapeno, onion, and garlic and cook until the onion is translucent.
8. Add your bone broth and corn to the pot and cook over medium heat.
9. Drain and rinse your beans and add to the pot as well.
10. Once chicken is cooked, shred and add to your pot.
11. Let simmer on low for 1½ hours, stirring occasionally.
12. With 30 minutes remaining, add 1 cup of heavy cream. Continue to stir occasionally.

YIELDS · 6-8 servings

SIMPLE PRESSURE COOKER BONE BROTH

Not only do I live on a farm now with my husband and son, but I've lived on a farm most of my life, so I know what it means not to waste anything. When we harvested our meat birds this past year, we knew we wanted to honor the animal and thank the Lord by putting as much of the bird to use as possible. So, I began a "routine" of sorts. We would cook a whole chicken, and then we would take the carcass and make nutrient dense (and oh-so-flavorful) bone broth. This recipe makes the most flavorful broth you've ever had! I use this in every recipe that calls for broth of any kind, and the flavor is unmatched.

PREP TIME · 30 minutes

COOK TIME · 4 hours

- 2½ pounds leftover poultry or meat bones (or purchased from your local butcher or meat department of your grocery store)
- 2 medium carrots, chopped
- 2 medium celery stalks, chopped
- 1 medium Vidalia onion, chopped
- 6 cloves garlic, chopped
- 1 teaspoon each of desired herbs
- 1 tablespoon apple cider vinegar
- 2 teaspoons black peppercorn
- 1 teaspoon salt
- Water (fill to max line)

INSTRUCTIONS

1   Place the meat bones in your pressure cooker.

2   Add in all other ingredients.

3   Fill the pressure cooker with water up to the max line.

4   Lock the lid, and set the steam release knob to the sealing position.

5   Press the "manual button" and set to high pressure for 120 minutes.

6   Once it is finished, and if you desire a more gelatinous broth, you can press the "manual button" and set to low pressure and cook for another 120 minutes.

7   Allow the pressure to naturally release—meaning wait on the pressure indicator to go down on its own before opening the lid (versus moving the steam release knob to the venting position).

8   Strain the liquid into jars of your choice.

9   You can use the broth for soups and other dishes that call for broth, or you can enjoy a nice, hot cup of broth between meals.

10 Make sure to salt to taste.

YIELDS · 96 ounces

CHICKEN-CASHEW-PINEAPPLE PASTA SALAD

Karen

I invented this when I tried to mimic a recipe from one of our favorite local eateries in the town where we lived when we were first married. Makes a pretty and tasty light summer lunch. We like to serve it with breadsticks, just like they did at the restaurant. (See our Buttery Soft Parmesan-Herbed Breadsticks *recipe on page 144.)*

PREP TIME · 25 minutes

- 16 ounces dry rotini pasta
- 1¼ cups mayonnaise (don't use salad dressing)
- 5 tablespoons buttermilk
- ¾ teaspoon season salt
- ½ teaspoon freshly cracked black pepper
- 2 teaspoons sugar
- 2 teaspoons white vinegar
- ¾ cup frozen green peas, thawed
- 2 cups chopped, cooked chicken
- ¼ cup purple onion, finely minced
- ½ cup fresh pineapple, finely chopped
- 1 cup salted cashew halves

INSTRUCTIONS

1. Bring a pot of water to a boil and cook rotini until it is just past al dente.

2. Drain into a colander and rinse with cold water.

3. While pasta is cooking, in a small bowl, combine mayonnaise, buttermilk, salt, pepper, sugar, and vinegar.

4. Place cooked pasta in a large bowl and add in peas, chicken, onion, and pineapple and mix until well blended.

5. Pour mayonnaise mixture evenly over the salad and mix gently until well incorporated.

6. Cover and refrigerate for at least 2 hours.

7. Just before serving, lightly stir in cashews.

YIELDS · 6-8 servings

COBB SALAD

Salads are usually not my thing—I am a meat and potatoes kind of girl. (Hey, I'm Southern, what do you expect?) But I have always enjoyed a good Cobb salad! Make it with fresh produce from your local farmer's market, and you have a real treat! I am obsessed with lemons, and I make sure to add lemon balm leaves fresh from my herb garden to my salad for subtle zest!

PREP TIME · 15 minutes

- 8 ounces chicken breast, cooked and diced
- 8 slices bacon, cooked and chopped
- 4 large hard-cooked eggs, peeled and chopped
- 9 cups butterhead lettuce, chopped
- 1 cup lemon balm leaves, chopped
- 1 medium cucumber, halved and thinly sliced
- 4 ounces black cherry tomatoes, cut in half
- 4 ounces crumbled blue cheese
- 1 large avocado, diced
- 4 tablespoons desired dressing

SOUL SOOTHER

Consuming lemon balm has been shown to decrease feelings of anxiousness, nervousness, and stress. It has also been shown to increase mood, attention, and cognitive function. It also can help with sleep/symptoms of insomnia, indigestion, nausea, and more!

INSTRUCTIONS

1. Add your greens to a large serving bowl.

2. Add the eggs and all other toppings to the serving bowl.

3. Toss your salad, add your favorite dressing, and enjoy!

YIELDS · 8 servings

CUCUMBER SALAD

Macey

I credit my dear friend, Elle, with this delicious recipe. I told her how I wanted to love cottage cheese so badly because of the health benefits, and she recommended incorporating cottage cheese into a dish I already love. Thus, this recipe was born! Thanks, Elle!

PREP TIME · 15 minutes

- 2 medium cucumbers, peeled and sliced
- 2 large tomatoes, diced
- 1 teaspoon salt
- 1 teaspoon pepper
- ½ to 1 cup cottage cheese (or feta cheese)

INSTRUCTIONS

1   Place cucumber and tomatoes in a large serving bowl.

2   Add salt, pepper, and cottage cheese. You can substitute feta cheese instead, if desired.

3   Toss to combine and serve.

YIELDS · 2 servings

The generous will prosper; those who refresh others will themselves be refreshed.

PROVERBS 11:25 (NLT)

EGG SALAD

This recipe is another delicious way to use farm fresh eggs from our laying hens—thanks ladies! I remember my dad making egg salad all of the time when I was growing up. I loved when he made it for me because it felt like such a treat each and every time, even though the recipe itself was easy. So, this is a reminder that the simple activities are truly the best memories with your family and friends, and this recipe is a tribute to my daddy and all of our special memories through every season! Cheers to many more!

PREP TIME · 10 minutes

COOK TIME · 12-15 minutes

- 4 pieces bacon, cooked and chopped
- 16 eggs, boiled and peeled
- ¼ cup spicy mayonnaise (see *Spicy Mayonnaise* recipe on page 226)
- ¾ cup plain mayonnaise
- 1 tablespoon dried dill
- 1 tablespoon spicy brown mustard
- 3 ounces bread and butter pickles, finely chopped

INSTRUCTIONS

1 Place eggs in a large bowl and mash with a fork until at a desired consistency.

2 Add all other ingredients and mix well.

3 If it is too dry, continue to add more mayonnaise until it reaches the desired consistency.

4 We love to make open faced egg salad sandwiches which makes the meal go a bit further as far as servings!

YIELDS · 4-6 servings

GRANNY BREWER'S POTATO SALAD

Macey

My Granny Brewer is an amazing cook. Her potato salad is one of my all-time favorite dishes that she makes, and I get extra helpings of it whenever I can. I love that she takes requests, especially during holiday seasons, and my dad and I make sure that we ask for this! When I called her to ask for the specific recipe, her words were, "I don't know how to write it down. I'll just have to explain it to you." That's the mark of a good recipe!

PREP TIME · 30 minutes

COOK TIME · 15 minutes

- 6 medium to large Yukon gold potatoes, diced into ½ inch cubes
- 5 eggs, boiled and finely chopped
- 3 ounces bread and butter pickles, finely chopped
- 1 cup mayonnaise
- 1 teaspoon spicy brown mustard
- ½ teaspoon dried dill
- Salt to taste
- Pepper to taste
- ½ teaspoon Cajun seasoning (optional)

INSTRUCTIONS

1 Put potatoes in a large pot, fill with water covering your potatoes, and bring to a boil.

2 Allow to boil for 10 to 15 minutes until fork tender.

3 Chop your eggs and bread and butter pickles.

4 Add your potatoes, eggs, pickles, mayonnaise, and mustard to a large serving bowl.

5 Mix until combined.

6 Add your dill, salt, pepper, and Cajun seasoning (if desired).

7 Stir until combined.

8 You may need to add more of any of these ingredients based on consistency and preference.

YIELDS · 4-6 servings

VEGETABLES &SIDES

"What I say is that, if a man really likes potatoes, he must be a pretty decent sort of fellow."

— A. A. MILNE

"Make sure to eat your vegetables!" Mama always said. Well, mama was right! And the dishes in this section will be just right for you if you want to serve up some delicious vegetables and other dishes to those you love. These scrumptious sides are sure to both satisfy the stomach and warm the heart.

GRANDMA MARGARET'S AU GRATIN POTATOES

Karen

My mom cooked for her entire life. When she was young, she learned from working in a German restaurant. Once married, she was the "lunch lady" at our local elementary school. Then, she was a cook at our city's hospital for nearly 40 years before retiring at the age of 81. This was one of the first recipes she taught me to make. A 1980's Midwestern classic. It goes great with beef, pork, poultry, or even fish.

PREP TIME · 25 minutes

COOK TIME · 1 hour 20 minutes

- 3 tablespoons butter
- 3 tablespoons all-purpose flour
- 2 cups of half-and-half
- 2 teaspoons salt
- ½ teaspoon black pepper
- 2 cloves of garlic, minced
- 1 small onion, minced
- 1¾ cups grated Gruyere cheese, divided
- ¾ cup of shredded sharp cheddar cheese, divided
- 5 medium Yukon Gold potatoes

INSTRUCTIONS

1   Preheat the oven to 400 degrees.

2   In a medium saucepan, melt the butter.

3   Whisk in the flour until smooth.

4   Add half-and-half, salt, pepper, and garlic to a simmer on low heat and cook for 10 minutes, stirring constantly with a whisk.

5   Remove from the heat and stir in 1¼ cups of the Gruyere and ½ cup of the cheddar cheeses.

6   Peel and slice potatoes to about ¼ inch thickness and place half of them in a greased casserole dish or cast-iron pan.

7   Spoon in half of the sauce, covering potatoes well.

8   Repeat with the rest of the potatoes and remaining sauce.

9   Top with remaining cheese.

10 Cover the pan with a piece of aluminum foil.

11 Bake for 25 minutes.

12 Remove the foil and bake for another 25 to 30 minutes, until lightly golden.

13 Remove from the oven and let cool for 15 minutes until sauce thickens back up.

YIELDS · 6 servings

MACEY'S MACARONI AND CHEESE

Macey

FUN FACT: My first ever published recipe was in the Ocmulgee Christian Academy cookbook, "Our Best Home Cooking," circa 1994, and the recipe was macaroni and cheese! I "submitted it" when I was only two years old (thanks mama!), and it featured just two ingredients—cheese and noodles! I've come a long way since then with a recipe that's still simple yet packed with even more cheesy goodness!

PREP TIME · 5 minutes
COOK TIME · 30 minutes

- 16 ounces of your favorite noodles, uncooked
- 2 tablespoons all-purpose flour
- 1 teaspoon sea salt
- 1 teaspoon garlic powder
- 4 tablespoons salted butter
- 2 cups whole milk
- ½ cup sour cream or Greek yogurt
- 5 cups shredded cheddar cheese, divided

INSTRUCTIONS

1 Cook noodles according to package instructions. We love to use conchiglie pasta; they look like conch shells.

2 Drain, rinse with cold water, and set aside.

3 Mix flour, salt, and garlic powder in a small bowl. Set aside.

4 In a saucepan over medium heat, melt the butter.

5 Add the flour mixture and whisk constantly to combine.

6 Cook for 1 minute until the mixture is slightly brown.

7 Add milk 1 cup at a time and whisk until the mixture is smooth.

8 Add sour cream (or yogurt) and whisk until smooth.

9 Cook until the mixture is thickened, about 3 to 5 minutes. Do not let it boil.

10 Once the mixture has thickened, reduce the heat to low and add 3 cups of cheese.

11 Stir until the cheese is melted and the mixture is smooth.

12 Pour your macaroni and cheese into a 9 x 13-inch baking dish.

13 Top with remaining cheese.

14 Broil on low until the cheese on top is slightly brown, about 3 to 5 minutes.

YIELDS · 6-8 servings

SWEET VEGGIE STIR FRY

I love this recipe, especially during harvest season when I have an abundance of these vegetables in my garden. I never get tired of this delectable combination, and it's such an easy and delicious way to use our produce!

PREP TIME · 15 minutes

COOK TIME · 15 minutes

- 2 tablespoons butter
- ½ pound sweet carrots, chopped
- ½ pound sweet potatoes, diced
- 1 Vidalia onion, diced
- ¼ to ½ cup maple syrup

INSTRUCTIONS

1 Melt butter in a large saucepan over medium heat.

2 Add in all vegetables and maple syrup.

3 Cook until desired doneness, about 15 to 20 minutes.

YIELDS · 6-8 servings

SOUL SOOTHER

Talk about creativity! This tri-colored carrot recipe is a winner in that category! Did you know that being creative positively impacts our mental health? Being creative can lead to an increase in positive emotions, reduce feelings and symptoms of depression and anxiety, and can strengthen our immune systems! So, find a way to get creative today!

MISS MEG'S FAMOUS FRIED RICE

Macey

Megan is my best friend of 27 years. We've done much, if not most, of life together. We have been there for the highs and the lows. We were the maid and matron of honor at each other's weddings. We lived together for a portion of college and spent practically every weekday together, if not the weekends as well. We didn't cook many meals in college, deciding to eat out much more often, but she cooks some amazing fried rice! Give her recipe a try; you won't regret it!

PREP TIME · 5 minutes

COOK TIME · 10 minutes

- 1¾ cups cooked white rice (best if cooked the day before)
- ¼ to ½ cup bone broth (if warming rice on the stove)
- 1 green onion/scallion
- 2 slices steak
- 3 tablespoons olive oil, divided
- 1 large egg
- ½ teaspoon salt
- ⅛ teaspoon black pepper
- 2 teaspoons soy sauce or coconut aminos

Do not neglect to do good and to share what you have,

for such sacrifices are pleasing to God.

HEBREWS 13:16 (ESV)

INSTRUCTIONS

1 Heat rice in the microwave or warm on the stovetop in a pot with bone broth until it's room temperature or slightly warm.

2 Cut the white part of the green onion into rounds and the green part diagonally. Keep the white and green parts separate and set aside. Reserve a few green slices for garnish.

3 Chop 2 slices of steak into square pieces about ¼ inch wide.

4 Cook separately in a saucepan in 1 tablespoon of olive oil and set aside.

5 Crack and whisk 1 large egg in a bowl.

6 Heat a large frying pan on medium high heat.

7 Once it's hot, add 1 tablespoon of your olive oil and swirl it around until it coats the entire surface of your pan.

8 Add the beaten egg to the hot pan.

9 With the blunt end of a spatula, swirl the loosely set egg around the pan to keep it fluffy while continuing to cook it.

10 When the bottom of the egg is set but the top is still running and not fully cooked, transfer it to a plate.

11 Add an additional tablespoon of olive oil to the pan.

12 Then, add the white part of the chopped green onion.

13 Stir fry and coat well with the oil.

14 Add the cooked and cooled rice to the pan.

15 With the spatula, use a slicing motion to separate the rice clumps without mashing or breaking the rice grains. Continue to toss the rice so it is coated with oil.

16 Add the cooked egg back to the pan and break it into smaller pieces while you combine it with the rice, and then add your cooked steak pieces.

17 Season with salt, pepper, and add your soy sauce or coconut aminos.

18 Toss to distribute.

19 Add the green part of the chopped green onion.

20 Taste your rice and add seasoning if needed.

21 Transfer it to a bowl and enjoy!

YIELDS · 2 servings

LOADED BRUSSELS BAKE

Macey

I've not always been a huge fan of brussels sprouts or cottage cheese by themselves, but I know that they are good fuel for my body. So, I was determined to like them. One day, I decided to put them together, and wow! My taste buds were amazed! Now, I make this dish at least once a month, and I think you'll find this to be a staple side dish in your home as well!

PREP TIME · 15 minutes

COOK TIME · 25 minutes

- 6 strips bacon, cooked and chopped
- 1 pound brussels sprouts
- 5 ounces cottage cheese (or feta cheese)
- 1 tablespoon coconut aminos
- 2 tablespoons extra-virgin olive oil
- Salt to taste
- Pepper to taste

INSTRUCTIONS

1 Preheat your oven to 425 degrees.

2 Line a large baking sheet with parchment paper and prepare your brussels sprouts by slicing off the nubby ends and removing any discolored or damaged leaves.

3 Cut each sprout in half from the top to the base.

4 In a bowl, combine your sprouts, cheese, coconut aminos, olive oil, salt, and pepper. Toss to combine.

5 Arrange in an even layer.

6 Roast until the sprouts are tender and deeply golden, about 17 to 25 minutes.

7 Remove the baking sheet from the oven and sprinkle bacon on top.

YIELDS · 4-6 servings

ROASTED TRICOLOR CARROTS WITH WHIPPED FETA, CRANBERRIES, & PINE NUTS

Karen

This is our family's new favorite holiday side dish that ends up looking like an award-winning dish from a cooking show! Try it for Easter, Thanksgiving, or for a festive birthday side dish.

PREP TIME · 15 minutes

COOK TIME · 45-50 minutes

- 2 pounds whole tri-color carrots, tops removed and lightly peeled
- 3 tablespoons extra virgin olive oil
- 3 tablespoons honey
- 1 medium lemon, juiced and zested
- ½ teaspoon salt
- Fresh ground black pepper, to taste
- 1 teaspoon ground cinnamon
- 6 ounces feta cheese, crumbled
- ⅓ cup plain full-fat Greek yogurt (or sour cream)
- 2 tablespoons honey, plus more for drizzling
- ¼ cup dried cranberries
- ¼ cup pine nuts

INSTRUCTIONS

1   Preheat the oven to 400 degrees.

2   Toss carrots in olive oil and 3 tablespoons honey and roast on a parchment paper lined baking sheet (or one sprayed with cooking spray) for 30 minutes, stirring occasionally.

3   While the carrots are roasting, make the whipped feta. In a food processor or blender, place the feta, Greek yogurt, 2 tablespoons honey, and zest from the lemon. Process on low until whipped smooth.

4   After the carrots have roasted for 30 minutes, remove from the oven.

5   Squeeze juice from 1 lemon over the carrots and top with salt, freshly ground black pepper, and cinnamon.

6   Toss well and return to the oven.

7   Decrease heat to 350 degrees and cook for another 15 to 20 minutes until lightly charred.

8   When carrots are done, spread whipped feta onto a serving platter.

9   Top with roasted carrots.

10   Sprinkle with cranberries, pine nuts, and a final drizzle of honey and serve.

YIELDS · 6 servings

MISS DEANN'S WORLD FAMOUS BBQ BAKED BEANS

Macey

This is my mom's most requested recipe. Everyone loves when she brings this dish to the potluck! She has tweaked it over the years, and it's aged like fine wine—it just keeps getting better! I'm honored that she shared it with me to share with you!

PREP TIME · 30 minutes

COOK TIME · 3-4 hours

- 4 or 5 boneless pork chops, cut into bite sized pieces
- 1 large Vidalia onion, chopped
- 4 tablespoons butter, divided
- ¾ cup packed brown sugar
- ⅓ cup ketchup
- 3 tablespoons spicy brown mustard
- ¼ cup honey
- 3 tablespoons Worcestershire sauce
- 1 tablespoon garlic salt
- ½ teaspoon cayenne pepper
- ½ teaspoon hot sauce
- 2 tablespoons blackstrap molasses
- Salt to taste
- Pepper to taste
- 1 pound bacon, cooked and crumbled
- 1 can (15 oz.) of pinto beans, drained and rinsed
- 1 can (15 oz.) of navy beans, drained and rinsed
- 1 can (15 oz.) of black beans, drained and rinsed
- 1 can (15 oz.) of light red kidney beans, drained and rinsed
- 1 can (15 oz.) of dark red kidney beans, drained and rinsed
- 1 can (15 oz.) of large white butter beans, drained and rinsed
- 8 ounces frozen lima beans
- Large and deep cast iron pan or Dutch oven

1 Preheat your oven to 350 degrees.

2 Sauté chopped onion and pork chop in 2 tablespoons butter until onion is translucent and pork is cooked thoroughly. Set aside.

3 Use the remaining butter to coat the bottom and sides of a large cast iron pan.

4 Heat the cast iron pan on the stove until warm, about 5 minutes.

5 Add brown sugar, ketchup, mustard, honey, Worcestershire sauce, garlic salt, cayenne pepper, hot sauce, molasses, salt, and black pepper to your cast iron pan and simmer for about 5 minutes on medium heat.

6 Add beans to the mixture in the cast iron pan and stir.

7 Add pork chops, onion, and bacon to your pan and stir.

8 Cook at 350 for 1 hour.

9 Reduce the oven to 250 degrees and cook for 3 hours, covered.

10 Stir the mixture occasionally.

11 Remove from the oven being careful to use oven gloves as the pan will be very hot.

YIELDS · 4-6 servings

BAKED CORNBREAD PUDDING

Karen

This is my family's favorite holiday side dish. You may assemble it the day before and keep it in the fridge, covered, until ready to bake. I always double the recipe, place it in a 9 x 13-inch pan and extend the baking time 15 to 20 more minutes until done.

PREP TIME · 10 minutes

COOK TIME · 45-60 minutes (or longer if doubling the recipe)

- 1 can (14.75 oz.) cream style corn
- 1 can (15 oz.) whole corn, drained
- 8 ounces sour cream
- ⅓ cup sugar
- ½ cup olive oil
- 2 eggs, lightly beaten
- 1 box (8.5 oz.) Jiffy corn muffin mix

INSTRUCTIONS

1 In a large bowl, mix all together and pour into a 2½ quart greased baking dish.

2 Bake at 350 degrees for 45 minutes to 1 hour until lightly golden.

3 If it begins to brown too quickly, cover the top lightly with foil for the last few minutes.

YIELDS · 4-6 servings

Hospitality Hack

If you want to offer hospitality, but don't want to be responsible for the whole meal, hold a baked potato bar. You provide baked potatoes, wrapped in foil and kept warm in a slow cooker. Guests can bring various toppings including chili, cooked broccoli, taco meat, cheese, sour cream, salsa, or sautéed onions and green peppers. Make a buffet line and everyone can fix a potato to their liking. For dessert, serve an assortment of jumbo cookies.

MAMA KAREN'S CALICO BAKED BEANS

Karen

And now, for a Midwest version of baked beans. I have taken these to numerous family picnics and church pot-lucks over the years and they always elicit "oohs" and "ahhs" as people go back for a second helping. A classic side dish that is popular in the summer but can be served year-round.

PREP TIME · 25 minutes
COOK TIME · 1 hour 30 minutes

- ½ pound center cut bacon, diced (may use precooked, crumbled turkey or chicken bacon)
- ½ yellow onion, diced
- ½ green bell pepper, thinly sliced into 1-inch strips
- ½ red bell pepper, thinly sliced into 1-inch strips
- 1 clove garlic, minced
- ¾ cup ketchup
- ⅓ cup barbecue sauce
- ¼ cup molasses
- 1 Tabasco sauce
- ¾ cup brown sugar, packed
- 1 teaspoon coarse ground black pepper
- 2 tablespoons Worcestershire sauce
- 2 tablespoons yellow mustard
- 2 cans (15 oz.) red beans, drained and rinsed
- 1 can (15 oz.) pinto beans, drained and rinsed
- 1 can (15 oz.) great Northern beans, drained and rinsed
- 1 can (15 oz.) butter beans, drained and rinsed

INSTRUCTIONS

1. Preheat the oven to 375 degrees.
2. In a large skillet, cook the bacon on medium high heat.
3. Remove from the stove and let cool.
4. Drain most of the fat off and then add the onion and peppers to the skillet and cook for about 8 minutes over medium-high heat or until it begins to caramelize.
5. Remove from heat.
6. In a large mixing bowl, combine the bacon mixture and the rest of the ingredients except for the beans and mix well.
7. Gently stir in the beans, being careful not to crush the butter beans.
8. Pour the mixture into a greased 9 x 13-inch baking pan and bake, covered with foil, for 1 hour.
9. Uncover and bake for an additional 20 to 30 minutes or until thickened.

YIELDS · About 10-12 servings

MR. JERRY'S BOILED PEANUTS

Macey

If you visit my family on any Saturday in the fall, you will find three things: a University of Georgia football game on the radio and television (with the television announcers muted…if you know, you know), a dove shoot happening in the field in front of our house, and boiled peanuts fresh from the field on the stove for the hunters. We snack on these peanuts all day, and they are delicious hot or cold as leftovers the next day, if there are any! When I asked my dad about his recipe and the ratios of each, he said he used "a good bit of salt." Just make sure that you salt based on your preference.

PREP TIME · 10 minutes

COOK TIME · 40 minutes

- 5 cups fresh peanuts, shells on
- ½ cup salt, or to taste
- Water (to cover peanuts)

INSTRUCTIONS

1   Wash your fresh peanuts in a colander making sure all dirt is removed.

2   Place peanuts in a large pot and cover with water.

3   Bring to a boil.

4   Add ½ cup of salt on top of your peanuts. Do NOT stir to incorporate initially.

5   Boil for 30 to 40 minutes or until done.

6   After about 10 minutes, you can stir occasionally.

7   We dip some out after about 25 minutes to taste and see if the peanuts are done and if they are salty enough.

YIELDS · 4 servings

TODD'S OVEN ROASTED CORN ON THE COB

Karen

My husband, Todd, and I discovered this way of preparing corn on the cob last summer and now we never make it any other way! The flavor is so intense because it isn't waterlogged due to boiling. Pick some corn up from a roadside stand when it is in season and try this. So delectable! And if you're in the Lansing, Michigan area, get your corn from Reese Farms on Wood Road—a fourth generation farm with the BEST sweet corn.

PREP TIME · 5 minutes

COOK TIME · 30-40 minutes

- 6 ears corn on the cob, husks and silks still on

INSTRUCTIONS

1 Preheat the oven to 350 degrees.

2 Place the cobs of corn, with their husks and silks still intact, on a baking sheet.

3 Roast in the oven for 30 minutes if the cobs are on the smaller side or 40 minutes if they are larger.

4 Remove from the oven and let cool until warm to the touch.

5 Hold the fat end of the cobs and peel back and remove the husks and silks.

6 Serve with butter, freshly ground sea salt, and freshly ground black pepper.

YIELDS · 6 servings

FRIED ONION RINGS

My mama loves fried onion rings. She always asks for this as a side with her meal instead of French fries, and her and my dad make the best fried onion rings I've ever tasted! I've watched them make these as I was growing up, and I think I've finally figured out how to replicate their recipe. FUN FACT: you can use a deep fryer for this recipe, or you can "shallow" fry as my mom would say! I'll show you the shallow fry method here. Happy frying!

PREP TIME · 15 minutes

COOK TIME · 15 minutes

- 2 medium Vidalia onions
- 3 cups all-purpose flour
- 3 teaspoons baking powder
- 1½ tablespoons garlic powder
- ¾ teaspoons onion powder
- 3 teaspoons seasoned salt
- 1½ teaspoons black pepper
- 1 teaspoon Cajun seasoning (optional)
- 4 eggs
- ¼ cup milk
- 1 cup extra virgin olive oil or avocado oil
- 1 to 2 teaspoons salt, divided

Hospitality Hack

Whether cooking for your family or for company, quality counts both in taste and in health. Choose fresh produce. Look for frozen and canned items that don't contain chemicals and additives. Buy organic, if cost effective. Think pure and unprocessed. For example, we love Redmond Real Salt. It is a pure, unrefined sea salt that is mined from an ancient seabed in Utah so it's safe from modern pollutants and full of trace minerals. We also love Ceylon cinnamon for its strong aroma and potent flavor and its blood sugar-lowering properties. Look closely at the labels and buy clean whenever you can.

INSTRUCTIONS

1 Prepare your onions by removing the skins and cutting off a small portion of each end of the onion.

2 Next, cut your onion so that you are left with "rings" by starting at one end and slicing downward in whatever thickness you desire to create rings.

3 Repeat this action until you reach the end of the onion.

4 Separate your rings by popping them out with your fingers.

5 Fill a large, deep cast iron pan with 1 cup of olive oil or avocado oil and heat oil over medium heat.

6 Combine flour, baking powder, garlic powder, onion powder, salt, pepper, and Cajun seasoning in a large bowl.

7 Whisk together until incorporated.

8 Next, crack 4 eggs into a bowl.

9 Add ¼ cup milk and stir until combined.

10 Take each ring and dip into your egg wash and then dip into your flour mixture.

11 For a thicker batter on your onion ring, repeat this process once more.

12 Working in batches, place rings in your cast iron pan once oil has reached desired temperature.

13 You should hear and see a sizzle when placing your onion rings in the cast iron pan. (You can test the warmth of the oil by dropping a small portion of the flour mixture into the oil and listening for the sizzle prior to placing your onion rings in the pan).

14 Fry until golden brown on each side, about 5 to 10 minutes.

15 Put a paper towel on a large plate, and then transfer onion rings to the plate to cool.

16 Salt with ½ teaspoon of salt each time that you take a new batch of onion rings out of your oil.

17 Serve hot and with your favorite dipping sauce!

YIELDS · 4-6 servings

MAPLE SWEET POTATO MASH

Karen

This fluffy and sweet side dish is something I created just before our youngest son left the nest to move to Australia. Unfortunately, the 2020 Covid pandemic hit and he had to move back to the states just a few months later. Eating some of mama's maple sweet potato mash made the transition a little easier. Serve this with poultry or ham for a fabulous comfort food side dish.

PREP TIME · 25 minutes

COOK TIME · 1 hour 20 minutes (or about 30 minutes if using the microwave)

- 6 large sweet potatoes
- 6 tablespoons salted butter
- ½ teaspoon vanilla extract
- ¼ teaspoon salt
- 1 teaspoon pumpkin pie spice
- ½ cup real maple syrup (do not use pancake syrup)
- ¼ cup chopped pecans
- 3 tablespoons brown sugar

INSTRUCTIONS

1 Preheat the oven to 375 degrees.

2 Prick potatoes and wrap in foil.

3 Bake for 1 hour until soft to the touch. (Or, prick and bake in the microwave on the potato setting until potatoes are cooked through.) Let potatoes cool until you can touch them without burning your hands.

4 Cut potatoes open and scoop out flesh and place in a greased casserole dish.

5 Add butter, vanilla, salt, and pumpkin pie spice to sweet potatoes and mash well.

6 Add maple syrup and stir.

7 Pop the dish into the oven for 15 minutes, uncovered.

8 Remove and set the oven to broil.

9 Top with pecans and sprinkle with brown sugar.

10 Broil for 3 to 5 minutes, watching closely so that it browns but does not burn.

YIELDS · 6 servings

GRANNY BREWER'S TURKEY DRESSING

Macey

Dressing is a Southern trademark, and every year as we come up on the Thanksgiving season, I simply cannot wait for my mama's and granny's turkey dressing. When I moved to Michigan, so many of my well-meaning family and friends tried to convince me that stuffing and dressing were the same thing! They are definitely not the same dish, and each deserves their own time in the limelight! Make sure to cook my Granny's dressing recipe and Karen's Classic Midwest Turkey Stuffing next time you are feeding a few. Both are simply delightful!

PREP TIME · 20 minutes

COOK TIME · 45-60 minutes

- 1 round (8 in.) of cornbread (see *Grandma Kit's Northern Cornbread* recipe on page 138)
- 4 slices of white bread, toasted
- 2 cups cooked, leftover chicken or turkey, chopped
- 2 medium Vidalia onions, finely chopped
- 6 boiled eggs, peeled and chopped
- 3 to 4 celery stalks, finely chopped
- 30 ounces of bone broth
- ½ teaspoon salt
- ¼ teaspoon pepper
- Avocado oil cooking spray

INSTRUCTIONS

1 Preheat your oven to 350 degrees.

2 Add all ingredients to a large mixing bowl and mix.

3 Prepare an 8 x 12-inch baking dish by spraying avocado oil on the bottom and sides.

4 Pour your batter in and bake for 45 minutes to an hour, until it is golden brown on top.

YIELDS · 6-8 servings

CLASSIC MIDWEST TURKEY STUFFING

Karen

This simple stuffing is a breeze to prepare. My mom used to stuff it inside of the turkey before baking—thus, the name stuffing. Then, she cooked her turkey inside of a brown paper grocery bag just like she learned from watching a local television culinary favorite, The Martha Dixon Show *in Lansing, Michigan. I prefer to make my stuffing in a buttered casserole dish instead. The blend of herbs and vegetables makes this savory dish a crowd-pleasing attraction.*

PREP TIME · 20 minutes

COOK TIME · 30-45 minutes

- ¾ cup butter
- 2 cups finely chopped onions
- 2 cups finely minced celery
- ½ cup finely chopped carrots
- 4 teaspoons dried sage
- 2½ teaspoons salt
- 1¼ teaspoons dried savory
- 1 teaspoon dried marjoram
- 1 teaspoon garlic powder
- 1 teaspoon black pepper
- ½ teaspoon dried thyme
- 14 cups ½-inch bread cubes, about 2 loaves of bread
- 1 cup chicken broth

INSTRUCTIONS

1. Preheat the oven to 325 degrees.

2. Melt the butter in a frying pan over low heat.

3. Add onions, celery, carrots, sage, salt, savory, marjoram, garlic powder, pepper, and thyme and sauté for 10 minutes.

4. Place bread cubes and the onion mixture in a large bowl, mixing until the bread is well coated.

5. If cooking in a dish, add about 1 cup chicken broth to moisten the bread cubes.

6. Then bake uncovered in a large, greased casserole dish at 325 degrees for 40 to 45 minutes.

7. If it browns too much, cover lightly with foil for the last few minutes.

8. If you are using this to stuff a turkey, omit the chicken broth, stuff in the turkey's cavity, and cook according to the turkey's directions.

YIELDS · 6-8 servings

PRESSURE COOKER MASHED POTATOES

My husband loves mashed potatoes and is wary when I use my pressure cooker for his favorite recipes. I've "diagnosed" him as a foodie, and he definitely prefers quality over convenience. This mashed potato recipe is so good that he prefers it over any other way to make it! Beware—the Ehman household loves butter and dairy so there's plenty found in this recipe! Foodie husband approved!

PREP TIME · 10 minutes

COOK TIME · 20 minutes

- 3 pounds Yukon gold potatoes, diced with skins on
- Water (to cover potatoes)
- 3 teaspoons salt
- ½ cup butter
- ¼ cup sour cream
- ¼ cup milk
- ½ teaspoon garlic powder
- 1 teaspoon Cajun seasoning
- ½ teaspoon pepper

INSTRUCTIONS

1   Place your trivet in the pressure cooker and add your potatoes.

2   Cover the potatoes with water.

3   Place the lid on the pressure cooker and set the venting knob to seal.

4   Cook on manual pressure on high for 8 minutes.

5   When the timer goes off, turn the pressure cooker off.

6   Quick release the pressure from the pot.

7   Drain the potatoes and then return to the pressure cooker.

8   Take a fork and mash your potatoes to the desired consistency.

9   Add in remaining ingredients and mix well.

YIELDS · 4-6 servings

PRESSURE COOKER CORN ON THE COB

Macey

Pressure cooking is such an easy and quick way to cook corn without making it soggy. Set your timer, walk away, and come back to delicious corn on the cob! Make sure to slather with butter and sprinkle with salt!

PREP TIME · 10 minutes
COOK TIME · 10 minutes

- 4 medium cobs of corn
- 1½ cups water
- 4 tablespoons butter, divided
- 1 teaspoon salt, divided

INSTRUCTIONS

1. Prepare your corn by cutting off the nubby end.

2. Remove the husk and silk peeling them from the end that you cut to the tip of the cob. I use a dry brush to remove as much silk as possible.

3. Pour 2 cups of water in your pressure cooker.

4. Place your trivet inside your pressure cooker and then place your ears of corn on the trivet.

5. Close the lid and put the venting knob in the sealing position.

6. Pressure cook for 2 minutes on high pressure.

7. Turn the venting knob to venting and allow the floating valve to drop before opening the lid. Be careful of the steam when opening the lid to your pressure cooker.

8. Remove corn with tongs and place on plates.

9. Rub each corn cob with 1 tablespoon butter and salt with ¼ teaspoon of salt.

10. Add more butter and salt as desired.

YIELDS · 4 servings

PRESSURE COOKER RICE

As a busy wife, mom, counselor, and professor, I need recipes in my arsenal that are quick and easy. My pressure cooker rice recipe is just that! Not only is it easy, but you do not sacrifice quality for convenience. It's the best of both worlds!

PREP TIME · 5 minutes
COOK TIME · 20 minutes

- 2 cups rice
- 2 cups bone broth (see *Simple Pressure Cooker Bone Broth* recipe on page 69)
- 1 teaspoon salt
- 1 tablespoon vinegar

INSTRUCTIONS

1   Rinse your rice under cold water and gently scrub the rice with your fingertips in a circling motion.

2   Pour out the cloudy water and rinse.

3   Drain well. This prevents your rice from sticking together.

4   Add your rice, bone broth, salt, and vinegar to your pressure cooker.

5   Close your lid and turn the venting knob to the sealing position.

6   Pressure cook on high pressure for 5 minutes.

7   When time is up, allow it to naturally release for 10 minutes.

8   After that time, turn the venting knob to the venting position to release the remaining pressure.

9   Open the lid and stir so that the rice will not stick to the bottom of the pressure cooker.

YIELDS · 6-8 servings

MAIN DISHES &MEATS

"There is something profoundly satisfying about sharing a meal. Eating together, breaking bread together, is one of the oldest and most fundamentally unifying of human experiences."

— BARBARA COLOROSO

And now…the main event!! These hearty, stick-to-your-ribs dishes will take on a starring role in your meal. From meat-centered to veggie-laden—and everything in between—you can relax knowing your main dish will be both satisfying and delicious.

CHEDDAR STUFFED MEATLOAF

Karen

A Midwest Michigan classic with a nod to our neighboring state of Wisconsin—a delicious cheddar cheesy middle. Serve with Grandma Margaret's Au Gratin Potatoes *from this cookbook (page 79) and a leafy green salad.*

PREP TIME · 15 minutes

COOK TIME · 1 hour 15 minutes

- 1½ pounds extra-lean ground beef (I use 85% or 92% lean)
- 1 cup crushed saltine crackers (or dry quick oats)
- 2 eggs, lightly beaten
- 1 small onion, finely chopped
- 1 teaspoon salt
- ¼ teaspoon black pepper
- 1 cup barbecue sauce, divided
- ⅓ cup ketchup
- ¼ cup mustard
- ⅓ cup whole milk
- 6 slices extra-sharp cheddar cheese
- 2 tablespoons mustard
- ⅓ cup real maple syrup (not pancake syrup)

INSTRUCTIONS

1 Preheat the oven to 350 degrees.

2 Mix beef, crackers, eggs, onion, salt, pepper, ½ cup barbecue sauce, ketchup, mustard, and milk.

3 Press half of the mixture in a lightly greased loaf pan or casserole dish.

4 Press down in the center to make an indentation.

5 Fold cheese slices in half and place in the indentation and top with the rest of the meat mixture, making sure to seal around the edges well.

6 Cover with foil,

7 Bake at 350 degrees for 1 hour.

8 Remove foil and baste with a mixture of the remaining barbecue sauce, 2 tablespoons mustard, and the maple syrup.

9 Bake, uncovered, for 15 minutes more or until done.

YIELDS · 6-8 servings

CHEESY CHICKEN POT PIE

Karen

I have made this recipe countless times to take to a new neighbor, a family with a new baby, or someone who has had an illness or death in the family. Today, my daughter Kenna does the same thing, carrying on the tradition for those she loves. I have included my from-scratch crust recipe, but feel free to use refrigerated, roll-out crusts if time is tight.

PREP TIME · 10-30 minutes (depending on if using purchased or homemade crust)

COOK TIME · 1 hour

- 2 homemade crusts (see recipe on next page) *or* 2 roll-out refrigerated pie crusts (these usually come in a package of two)
- 2 cups chopped, cooked chicken
- 1½ cups extra sharp cheddar cheese, grated
- 1 can cream of chicken soup
- 1 bag (16 oz.) frozen vegetables for soup (Don't just use mixed vegetables. Find one that has potatoes in it too.)
- Salt and pepper, to taste

INSTRUCTIONS

1 Preheat the oven to 350 degrees.

2 Mix all but the crust in a large bowl, adding salt and pepper to taste.

3 Roll out 1 crust into a standard pie pan, leaving the edges hanging over.

4 Place ingredients from the bowl into the crust.

5 Roll out the second crust on top.

6 Use your fingers to crimp edges of both crusts tightly together to seal.

7 I like not to have crusts hang over the edge of the pan, but instead push them close to the pie so the edge of the pan still shows.

8 This prevents the edges of the crust from burning.

9 Bake at 350 degrees for 1 hour.

Note: If giving to someone, do *not* bake it but wrap it tightly in plastic wrap. Include instructions for them to remove the plastic wrap and bake it at 350 degrees for 1 hour. You can also freeze it in the plastic wrap. To bake, thaw completely and then bake at 350 degrees for 1 hour.

YIELDS · 8 servings

From-Scratch Pie Crust

- 2 cups unbleached flour (or a little more)
- 1 teaspoon salt
- Scant cup butter (about a teaspoon or two less than a cup) or you may use lard or butter-flavored shortening
- 6 to 8 tablespoons of water from melting ice—seriously, cold tap water will not work, so get out a bowl, fill it with ice and let it begin melting a while before you begin making the crust

INSTRUCTIONS

1   Mix flour and salt.

2   Cut in butter with a pastry blender (or a large fork.) Stir water in lightly to form a ball. DO NOT HANDLE TOO MUCH! It will make the dough tough, not flaky.

3   Divide in half and wrap one half in plastic wrap so it won't dry out and place it in the refrigerator.

4   Roll out the first crust on a well-floured counter with a well-floured rolling pin to make a circle just a bit bigger in diameter than your pie pan.

5   Repeat with the second crust when it is time to place the top on.

YIELDS · 2 pie crusts

DELICIOUS GLUTEN-FREE SALSA ENCHILADAS

There was a time when my husband needed to be gluten-free, until we discovered sourdough! So, I made it a point to find recipes that I could make that were also delicious when made gluten-free. We found the Siete™ brand during this time, and I decided to make enchiladas using Siete™ tortillas. We were pleasantly surprised to find that the dish didn't even taste gluten-free—a win in our book! Feel free to add or substitute your favorite "filling" for the enchiladas. You really can't go wrong!

PREP TIME · 15 minutes

COOK TIME · 20 minutes

- 2 tablespoons butter
- 1 pound ground beef
- 1 package taco seasoning (or see *Taco Seasoning Mix* recipe on page 228)
- 3 cups salsa
- 1 package gluten-free tortillas, about 12 tortillas
- 15-ounce can refried beans
- 15-ounce can of corn kernels
- 1½ cups shredded cheddar cheese, divided
- Avocado oil cooking spray

INSTRUCTIONS

1   Heat a medium saucepan over medium heat and melt 2 tablespoons of butter.

2   Add your ground beef and brown it.

3   Season the ground beef with taco seasoning. Set aside.

4   Preheat your oven to 350 degrees.

5   Prepare your large baking dish by spraying it with avocado oil.

6   Take 1 cup of salsa and spread on the bottom of the baking dish.

7   Take each gluten-free tortilla and put 1½ tablespoons of refried beans, 1½ tablespoons ground beef, 1 tablespoon of corn kernels, and about 1½ tablespoons of cheese.

8   Roll up your tortilla and place seam down in the baking dish.

9   Repeat until you cover the entire baking dish with rolled up, stuffed tortillas.

10   Cover with remaining salsa and then cheese.

11   Bake for about 20 minutes or until the cheese is slightly brown.

12   Allow to cool for a few minutes, and then serve!

YIELDS · 4-6 servings

SPICY MAYO POKE BOWL

Macey

When my husband and I moved to Tennessee from Michigan, we sorely missed several of our favorite restaurants. One of those restaurants was Ukai, and they had the best sushi we both have ever had. One day, we both wanted sushi so badly, and so I tried to recreate one of our favorite sushi rolls but made it into a bowl. Next time you're craving sushi but want to stay in, try this instead, and if you're ever in the Lansing area, make sure to stop by Ukai! Tell them the Ehmans sent you!

PREP TIME · 5 minutes

COOK TIME · 15 minutes

- 2 cups sushi rice, cooked (see *Pressure Cooker Rice* recipe on page 99)
- 2 tablespoons butter
- 1 pound shrimp
- 8 tablespoons spicy mayonnaise, divided (see *Spicy Mayonnaise* recipe on page 226)
- 4 tablespoons cream cheese, cut into 1 tablespoon cubes

- 4 teaspoons coconut aminos
- 4 teaspoons maple syrup
- 1 cup crab salad
- 2 medium avocados, diced
- 1 small cucumber, sliced
- 2 teaspoons sesame seeds

INSTRUCTIONS

1. In a medium saucepan, melt the butter.

2. Add your shrimp to the saucepan and cook 1 to 2 minutes on each side or until pink.

3. Next, place ½ cup of rice in each bowl.

4. Add 2 tablespoons of spicy mayonnaise, 1 tablespoon of cream cheese, 1 teaspoon of coconut aminos, and 1 teaspoon of maple syrup (my secret ingredient) to each bowl and stir to combine.

5. Top each bowl with ¼ cup of crab salad, ½ of an avocado, ¼ of a small cucumber, and ¼ pound of shrimp.

6. Sprinkle ½ teaspoon of sesame seeds and enjoy!

YIELDS · 4 servings

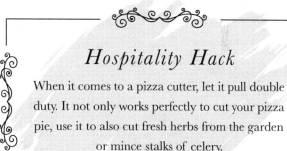

Hospitality Hack

When it comes to a pizza cutter, let it pull double duty. It not only works perfectly to cut your pizza pie, use it to also cut fresh herbs from the garden or mince stalks of celery.

THAI SHRIMP COCONUT CURRY

Macey

This recipe was inspired by my friend, Megan, when she and her mom, Angela, took me to eat Indian cuisine when we attended Georgia College and State University in Milledgeville, GA together. Before that day, I didn't even know what curry was! Yet that day in a restaurant in downtown Milledgeville, I discovered a love for Indian cuisine. So, I decided to make my own curry at home, and this recipe was a success!

PREP TIME · 15 minutes
COOK TIME · 15 minutes

- 2 tablespoons butter
- 1 pound raw large shrimp; thawed if frozen, peeled, and deveined
- 1 to 2 tablespoons avocado oil or olive oil
- 1 medium Vidalia onion, diced
- 1 medium bell pepper, cut into thin strips ½ inch long
- 2 large jalapenos, seeds removed and finely chopped
- 1 can (14 oz.) coconut milk
- 3 tablespoons red curry paste
- 1½ tablespoons coconut aminos
- 2 tablespoons brown sugar
- 2 tablespoons cornstarch
- 2 to 3 tablespoons basil
- ½ teaspoon red pepper flakes
- 1 teaspoon lime juice
- Cooked rice, for serving (see *Pressure Cooker Rice* recipe on page 99)

INSTRUCTIONS

1 Prep shrimp as needed.

2 Heat 2 tablespoons of butter in a medium saucepan.

3 When your saucepan is warm, add shrimp.

4 Cook for 1 to 2 minutes on each side until fully cooked. Set aside.

5 Add your oil to the same saucepan that you cooked your shrimp.

6 Over medium heat, add onion, bell peppers, and jalapenos and cook until softened, about 5 to 10 minutes.

7 Using a slotted spoon, transfer your vegetables to a bowl and set aside.

8 Over medium heat, add the coconut milk, red curry paste, coconut aminos, and brown sugar to the medium saucepan.

9 Whisk together and bring to a gentle boil.

10 Add cornstarch to your sauce and simmer until thickened, about 5 minutes.

11 Add your cooked shrimp and vegetables to the sauce.

12 Allow your curry to simmer gently, stirring occasionally, until you've reached your desired thickness.

13 Toward the end of cooking, add your basil, red pepper flakes, and lime juice.

14 Serve with rice.

YIELDS · 4 servings

SHEET PAN WHOLE CHICKEN AND VEGGIES

Macey

This is a recipe that I make very frequently in our home, especially since we butchered our meat chickens this past year and have an abundance of whole chickens in our freezer. We eat a baked chicken leg with a side of vegetables, and then, we use the leftover chicken to make chicken salad (see Chicken Salad *recipe on page 113). We use the leftover chicken carcass to make nutrient-dense bone broth (see* Simple Pressure Cooker Bone Broth *recipe on page 69), so this recipe keeps on giving!*

PREP TIME · 30 minutes

COOK TIME · 1 hour 15 minutes

- 1 whole chicken, approximately 4 to 5 pounds
- 4 large carrots, chopped
- 3 large Yukon gold potatoes, chopped
- 1 medium Vidalia onion, chopped
- 8 ounces mushrooms, diced
- ½ to 1 cup olive oil
- 2 tablespoons lemon juice
- ½ teaspoon garlic salt, divided
- ½ teaspoon Cajun seasoning
- 2 tablespoons parsley

Don't get tired of helping others.

You will be rewarded when the time is right, if you don't give up.

GALATIANS 6:9 (CEV)

INSTRUCTIONS

1 Preheat your oven to 430 degrees.

2 Line a large sheet pan with parchment paper.

3 Pat your chicken dry with a paper towel. Make sure to check the cavity of the bird and discard the neck, etc.

4 Place your chicken on the sheet pan.

5 Arrange the carrots, potatoes, and the onion around the chicken on the sheet pan, spreading evenly.

6 Drizzle the olive oil across the chicken and potatoes.

7 Brush lemon juice on the chicken and season with ¼ teaspoon of garlic salt and Cajun seasoning each.

8 Bake for 37 minutes.

9 Take the sheet pan out, and turn your chicken over using tongs.

10 Baste the chicken with ¼ cup of oil on the side that is now facing up.

11 Put ¼ teaspoon of garlic salt and Cajun seasoning on that side.

12 Add the diced mushrooms and stir your vegetables, and put the sheet pan back in the oven for another 37 minutes.

13 With 1 minute remaining, sprinkle your parsley on top of your chicken and vegetables.

14 Let cool for a few minutes, and then serve.

15 If using it for chicken salad, let it cool completely.

16 Pick the chicken off the carcass, shred, and store in an airtight container in your fridge.

YIELDS · 2-6 servings

SHEET PAN NACHOS

Macey

Sheet pan nachos are regularly featured on Taco Tuesday nights in our home. We love how simple and easy this recipe is and that we can whip it up in no time. We take the sheet pan to the table, gather around, and help ourselves straight from the pan! More than the ease of this recipe, I love how it brings my family together—literally and figuratively!

PREP TIME · 10 minutes
COOK TIME · 20 minutes

- 2 tablespoons butter
- ½ pound ground beef
- ½ pound ground venison
- 1 package taco seasoning (or see *Taco Seasoning Mix* recipe on page 228)
- 6 ounces tortilla chips (enough to cover sheet pan)
- 1½ cups shredded three cheese Mexican cheese
- 3 ounces black cherry tomatoes, halved
- 3 ounces pickled jalapenos
- 1 medium avocado
- 4 tablespoons salsa
- 4 tablespoons sour cream

INSTRUCTIONS

1. Heat butter in a medium pan over medium heat.
2. Brown your meat and season with taco seasoning. Set aside.
3. Turn your oven to broil on low.
4. Line a large baking sheet with parchment paper.
5. Spread your tortilla chips, covering the sheet pan.
6. Evenly distribute meat across your tortilla chips.
7. Next, sprinkle an even layer of cheese, tomatoes, and jalapenos across your chips and meat.
8. Put your sheet pan in the oven and cook until the cheese is melted and golden-brown, about 5 to 10 minutes.
9. Make sure to keep an eye on it so that it doesn't burn.
10. Once your nachos are cooked, take the sheet pan out of the oven and add your avocado, salsa, and sour cream.
11. Serve straight from the pan!

YIELDS · 4 servings

CHICKEN SALAD

Macey

When I asked my best friend, Megan, what I've cooked for her that was her favorite, she said two things—homemade sourdough pizza and chicken salad. Last summer, she came to the farm to help me when my dog, Luna, was very sick. I made some chicken salad prior to her visit, and she loved it so much that I packed her the rest to eat on her four-hour drive home. This is a great recipe to make for loved ones and to make for a road trip as well as a picnic! Frequently, my husband and I pack chicken salad for picnics to the Conasauga River along with our favorite chips or homemade sourdough sandwich bread.

PREP TIME · 15 minutes

- 2 to 3 cups cooked, shredded chicken
- ½ cup mayonnaise
- ½ cup spicy mayonnaise (see *Spicy Mayonnaise* recipe on page 226)
- 1 tablespoon spicy brown mustard
- 3 ounces bread and butter pickles, finely chopped
- 1 tablespoon dried dill

INSTRUCTIONS

1 Place cooked and shredded chicken into a serving bowl.

2 Add mayonnaise, spicy mayonnaise, and mustard. Stir to combine.

3 Add the bread and butter pickles and dried dill to the chicken mixture. Stir until all are incorporated.

4 You can eat it as is, eat it with your favorite chips, or make a chicken salad sandwich with homemade sourdough sandwich bread. Make it extra fun, and pack a picnic and go somewhere fun with your loved ones!

YIELDS · 2-4 servings

SOUL SOOTHER

Macey mentioned in the introduction to this recipe that her family frequently packs chicken salad and takes it on a picnic to the Conasauga River. They actually put their chairs in the shallow part of the river and dip their toes in the river as they eat. There are so many mental health benefits in this simple family activity: time in the sunshine, in nature, and grounding your body (which is your bare feet touching the earth). We highly encourage getting outside as a family!

MARIANGE'S CHICKEN PARMESAN SANDWICHES

Karen

This mouth-watering recipe is one our new daughter-in-law, Mariange, makes for our youngest son, Spencer. When they married a few months ago, we knew she was a beautiful soul, inside and out. Now we know she is also a fabulous cook! He can't get enough of this classic Italian dish turned hearty sandwich. NOTE: You may also serve the chicken with sauce and pasta instead of as a sandwich.

PREP TIME · 25 minutes

COOK TIME · 1 hour, or up to 2 hours for simmering the sauce

- 6 cloves of garlic, minced
- 1 cup of fresh basil, finely chopped
- ½ of a medium yellow onion, finely diced
- ¼ cup olive oil
- 8 ounces of tomato paste
- 1 can (28 oz.) crushed tomatoes
- Italian blend seasonings to taste (oregano, thyme, rosemary)
- 1 cup water
- 4 boneless skinless chicken breasts
- More Italian blend seasonings to taste (oregano, thyme, rosemary)
- 3 medium eggs, lightly beaten
- 1½ cups Italian breadcrumbs
- Vegetable oil for frying
- Minced garlic, to taste
- 4 tablespoons butter, softened
- ⅔ cup Parmesan cheese, divided
- 8 pieces soft French bread
- ⅓ cup fresh mozzarella

INSTRUCTIONS

1 To start the sauce, mince the garlic and add it to a large pot with the basil, diced onions, and olive oil.

2 Sauté until garlic is slightly golden, and then add tomato paste and stir.

3 Add crushed tomatoes, Italian seasonings to taste, and 1 cup of water or as needed so that the sauce isn't too thick.

4 Let that simmer uncovered on very low heat for at least 1 or up to 2 hours until done, stirring regularly.

5 When the sauce looks almost done, pound chicken breast to tenderize them so they are nice and flat.

6 Season chicken with some Italian seasoning blend.

7 After that, whisk together the eggs in a bowl, and set the bowl to the side.

8 Place breadcrumbs in another bowl, adding in more Italian seasoning to taste.

9 Dip chicken in eggs and then breadcrumb mixture. Repeat dipping in eggs and crumbs once more and set to the side to be fried!

10 Heat about an inch of vegetable oil in a deep skillet.

11 Fry the chicken, turning occasionally until no longer pink inside, about 15 to 18 minutes depending on the thickness.

12 While the chicken is frying, make the bread.

13 Mix garlic (to taste) with the softened butter.

14 Blend in ⅓ cup parmesan cheese.

15 Spread butter mixture evenly on one side of each of the bread slices and wrap in foil.

16 Bake at 375 degrees until the bread is nice and warm, about 20 minutes.

17 Assemble sandwiches, placing chicken on the bread, spreading sauce on the chicken and sprinkling with mozzarella and remaining Parmesan.

YIELDS · 4 servings

OVEN BAKED FALL-OFF-THE-BONE RIBS

FUN FACT: My very first school counseling job was in Vidalia, GA. I was there for about 2½ years until I married Mitchell and moved to Michigan. My mom would always send me Vidalia onion products from Herndon Farms as a care package every so often and at the holidays. It warmed my heart to cook with these products especially when I was missing my Georgia family and friends. One day, when I was making ribs, all I had on hand was a small amount of the Vidalia onion BBQ sauce and honey mustard. So I had to combine them to make this recipe work, and it was a beautiful combination! Hands down the best ribs I've ever had!

PREP TIME · 10 minutes

COOK TIME · 2 hours 30 minutes

- 2 large racks of ribs
- ½ cup brown sugar
- 4 drops liquid smoke
- 1 teaspoon salt
- 1 teaspoon pepper
- 1 tablespoon paprika
- 1 tablespoon garlic powder
- 1 cup Vidalia onion BBQ sauce
- 1 cup Vidalia onion honey mustard

Hospitality Hack

If you have leftover liquid, make sure to store it in an airtight container and use it for your next soup or any recipe where you need bone broth or meat stock! You'll impress all your loved ones or guests with a meal packed with extra flavor!

1   Preheat your oven to 300 degrees.

2   Remove the excess fat and the membrane by using a butter knife to separate the membrane from the ribs and by using a clean paper towel to pull the membrane away from the ribs.

3   Make the rub by mixing the brown sugar, liquid smoke, and the spices together.

4   Put your rub on each side of your ribs with your hands, ensuring every part of the meat is covered.

5   Cover a large sheet pan with parchment paper.

6   Put ribs on parchment paper.

7   Cover with tin foil.

8   Bake for 2 hours and 15 minutes.

9   Take the ribs out and brush with the BBQ sauce and honey mustard on both sides.

10 Put your ribs back in the oven uncovered and broil on low for 10 to 15 minutes keeping a watch on them so that they do not burn.

11 Take out and enjoy. Try not to fight over them!

YIELDS · 4 servings

MEMA'S SHEPHERD'S PIE

Macey

My great grandmother, Abbie, was an Elton before she married my great grandfather, Ralph Thomas. Her daughter, my Mema, always told me that the Eltons in England were members of parliament and that we were distantly related to a princess. I always dreamed that this recipe was handed down from generation to generation and came straight from England to Georgia, as did our ancestors. I love making this recipe now because it reminds me of fond memories with my grandmother and feels like an honor to her memory. Enjoy our twist on this authentic dish!

PREP TIME · 10 minutes
COOK TIME · 30 minutes

- 4 cups mashed potatoes (see *Pressure Cooker Mashed Potatoes* recipe on page 97)
- 1 tablespoon extra-virgin olive oil
- 1 pound ground beef or ground lamb
- 1 clove garlic, chopped
- 2 onions, finely chopped
- 2 medium carrots, finely chopped
- 2 stalks celery, finely diced
- ½ teaspoon salt
- ¼ teaspoon ground paprika
- Black pepper to taste
- 2 tablespoons all-purpose flour
- 2 tablespoons tomato paste
- 1½ cups bone broth
- 1 tablespoon parsley
- ½ teaspoon thyme
- 1 teaspoon rosemary
- 1 cup frozen peas
- 1 cup frozen corn kernels
- 1 pie crust (9 x 13-inch) to cover baking dish (see *Sourdough Pie Crust* recipe on page 192, or you can use a crust from frozen. If using a frozen crust, follow package directions.)
- 1 cup shredded sharp cheddar cheese
- Avocado oil cooking spray

INSTRUCTIONS

1   Preheat your oven to 400 degrees.

2   Heat the oil over medium high heat in a large, deep skillet.

3   Brown your ground beef or lamb and then add your chopped vegetables.

4   Saute until softened.

5   Sprinkle salt, paprika, pepper, and flour over the meat and vegetable mixture.

6   Cook for 2 minutes, stirring often.

7   Stir in tomato paste and cook, stirring constantly for about 1 minute.

8   Add your broth, herbs, peas, and corn and simmer for 4 to 5 minutes.

9   Spray your 9 x 13-inch baking dish with avocado oil cooking spray.

10 Put your pie crust in the baking dish ensuring that it covers the entire dish.

11 Pour your meat and vegetable mixture into the baking dish and spread evenly.

12 Spread your mashed potatoes on top of the filling. Do not mix.

13 Sprinkle with cheese.

14 Bake for 20 minutes or until golden.

15 You can put your baking dish on top of a sheet pan in case any of the filling bubbles out of the pan.

YIELDS · 6-8 servings

But be sure to fear the Lord and serve him faithfully with all your heart;
consider what great things he has done for you.

1 SAMUEL 12:24

MICHIGAN PASTY HAND PIES

Karen

My father, Pat Patterson, was a cook in the Navy during the Korean War. He later went on to have a lengthy career in catering and eventually owned his own restaurant in Lansing Michigan called Pat's Pantry. *He was famous for his homemade pasties. These meat and veggie hand pies were a staple of copper miners and lumberjacks that were brought to Michigan's upper peninsula from the mining region of Cornwell, England. Wives would fill a small circle of dough with leftover meat, potatoes, onions and rutabagas, and then fold the pastry over, sealing the edges to make a half-moon shape. Legend says miners would warm these tasty pasties on a shovel over their lantern candles. FUN FACT: Those who live in the upper peninsula of Michigan are called "Yoopers" from the initials "U.P." We who live downstate are known as trolls, because we live "under"—south of—the Mackinac Bridge.*

PREP TIME · 45 minutes (plus dough must chill at least 2 hours)

COOK TIME · 60-70 minutes

- 3 cups flour
- 1¼ cups (2½ sticks) butter, cold and cut into bits
- 1½ teaspoons salt
- ½ cup ice-cold water
- 1 pound lean ground beef, uncooked
- ¾ cups, peeled and finely chopped carrots (about ¼-inch cubes)
- 1 medium onion, finely chopped
- 3¾ cups potatoes, peeled and cut in small cubes (about ¼-inch cubes)
- ½ cup rutabaga, peeled and chopped (about ¼-inch cubes)
- 2 teaspoons salt
- ½ teaspoon black pepper
- 6 teaspoons butter

Hospitality Hack

Whenever preparing a main dish that freezes well, think of this phrase, "Cook once. Eat twice." What this means is that whenever you are preparing such a dish—perhaps lasagna or a chicken pot pie—double the recipe. Make one to prepare for dinner that night. Wrap the other one tightly in foil and store in the freezer. Then, when you have a busy day and no time to cook—or when unexpected company drops by—you will have a main dish you can simply thaw and pop into the oven.

INSTRUCTIONS

1   In a large bowl, combine flour, butter, and salt.

2   Blend until just combined and add water, 1 tablespoon at a time to form a dough.

3   Toss mixture until it forms a ball.

4   Knead dough for 5 minutes.

5   Wrap in plastic wrap and chill for 2 hours or more.

6   Preheat the oven to 375 degrees.

7   Combine raw meat with the remaining ingredients, except the butter, in a large bowl and mix well.

8   Divide the dough into 6 pieces.

9   On a lightly floured surface, roll one of the pieces into a 9- or 10-inch round.

10 Put about 1 cup of filling on half of the round.

11 Moisten the edges with water and fold the unfilled half over the filling to make a half-moon shape.

12 Pinch the edges together tightly and crimp them with the tines of a fork and prick all over the top with a fork.

13 Cut a 1-inch slit in the middle of the crust.

14 Repeat with remaining dough to make 5 more pasties.

15 Transfer them to a baking sheet lined with parchment paper or sprayed with cooking spray.

16 Bake in a 375-degree oven for 30 minutes.

17 Put 1 teaspoon butter through the slit in each pasty and continue baking for 30 minutes more.

18 Remove from the oven and cool for 15 minutes.

19 Serve with beef gravy or catsup, like we do here in The Mitten State (Michigan). Enjoy!

Note: These freeze well for up to one month.

YIELDS · 6 pasties

SPAGHETTI PIE

Karen

I have been making this recipe for over two decades and my family has never grown tired of it. You can assemble it the day before and cover tightly with foil before refrigerating. Then, when you are ready to bake it, simply pop it in the oven and extend the baking time by 5 minutes or so.

PREP TIME · 25 minutes

COOK TIME · 30 minutes

- 6 ounces dry spaghetti noodles
- $\frac{1}{4}$ cup Parmesan cheese
- 1 pound ground turkey sausage (or any ground sausage)
- $\frac{1}{3}$ cup chopped onion
- $\frac{1}{4}$ cup minced green pepper
- 3 tablespoons olive oil
- 2 eggs, lightly beaten
- $2\frac{1}{2}$ cups spaghetti or pasta sauce (I use Whole Foods 365™ Organic Marinara)
- $1\frac{1}{4}$ cup sour cream
- $1\frac{1}{2}$ cups Italian blend cheese (mozzarella, asiago, provolone, Romano, and Parmesan)

INSTRUCTIONS

1   Preheat the oven to 350 degrees.

2   Cook spaghetti noodles in boiling water according to directions.

3   Drain noodles and mix in a large bowl with the Parmesan cheese.

4   Allow to cool for 10 minutes.

5   Meanwhile, brown the sausage, onion, and green pepper in the olive oil.

6   Drain off excess liquid.

7   Next, add beaten eggs to the noodle mixture, stirring well.

8   Spray a 10-inch-deep dish pie pan with cooking spray and pat the noodle mixture in the bottom and up the sides, pressing well.

9   Add the spaghetti sauce to the browned, drained sausage mixture.

10   Stir in the sour cream and then spread mixture on top of the spaghetti, making sure it reaches all the way to the sides of the pan.

11   Bake at 350 degrees for 25 minutes.

12   Remove from the oven and sprinkle with the Italian cheese blend.

13   Return to the oven and broil for 2 to 3 minutes, just until the cheese becomes lightly golden and bubbly.

14   Let cool slightly before cutting into wedges.

YIELDS · 6 servings

VEGGIE LASAGNA

Karen

Not only is this vegetarian main dish scrumptious, it's super simple because you do not need to boil the lasagna noodles. Serve it with garlic bread and a crunchy salad and dinner is done!

PREP TIME · 20 minutes

COOK TIME · 1 ½ hours

- 2 tablespoons olive oil
- 4 ounces canned mushrooms, drained (or ⅓ cup sliced fresh)
- 1 small zucchini, sliced thin
- 1 small yellow summer squash, sliced thin
- 1 medium onion, chopped
- ½ a medium green pepper, diced
- 1 jar (32 oz.) pasta sauce (I use Rao's™ brand)
- 1½ cups water
- ¾ teaspoon salt
- ½ teaspoon pepper
- ¼ teaspoon grated nutmeg
- 12 uncooked regular lasagna noodles (not the no-boil type)
- 16 ounces whole milk ricotta cheese
- 12 ounces Italian blend shredded cheese (or mozzarella)
- 1 cup grated Romano cheese
- 2 teaspoons fresh minced garlic

INSTRUCTIONS

1 Preheat the oven to 350 degrees.

2 In a large fry pan, sauté the mushrooms, zucchini, squash, onion, and green pepper in the olive oil for 5 minutes.

3 In a large bowl, combine the sauce, water, salt, pepper, and nutmeg.

4 In another bowl, combine the ricotta cheese and garlic.

5 Spray a 9 x 13-inch pan with cooking spray.

6 Spread about 1 cup of sauce over the bottom.

7 Arrange 4 noodles over the sauce.

8 Cover the noodles with ⅓ of the vegetables, ⅓ of the remaining sauce, and then ⅓ of the ricotta cheese, ⅓ of the Italian blend, and then ⅓ of the Romano.

9 Repeat the layers twice more.

10 Make sure the last layer has any noodles well covered with sauce that are peeking out.

11 Seal with foil and bake at 350 degrees for 1½ hours.

12 Remove from the oven and remove the foil.

13 Let stand for 10 minutes until serving.

YIELDS · 9-12 servings

FOUR CHEESE MEAT LASAGNA

Macey

Shoutout to my friend and coworker, Lisa, who said that my lasagna was the best that she's ever tasted and the fact that she taste-tested most of my recipes for me while Karen and I were writing this cookbook! She had such a hard job—wink, wink! I believe this is one of her all-time favorites, and it's one of my all-time favorites too. I love anything that has ricotta cheese in it, and this dish definitely delivers! Dairy lovers, beware, this may be your new favorite dish to make!

PREP TIME · 10 minutes

COOK TIME · 45 minutes

- 8 ounces cottage cheese
- 8 ounces ricotta cheese
- 1 egg
- ½ cup raw grated Parmesan
- 3 cups shredded mozzarella, divided
- 1 teaspoon salt, divided
- 1 teaspoon Italian seasoning
- Pepper to taste
- 2 pounds ground beef
- 2 tablespoons butter
- 9 ounces lasagna noodles
- 3 cups water (enough to cover noodles)
- 28 ounces of marinara sauce
- Avocado oil cooking spray

Hospitality Hack

If space is an issue when it comes to opening your home, consider hosting during the warm summer months when you can eat outside on a picnic table. Children can even spread blankets on the grass and enjoy their meal. Or let a local park provide the location while you do the hosting. Pack up a basket of food and head to the park to visit with another family or group of singles from your church.

1 Preheat your oven to 350 degrees.

2 Mix cottage cheese, ricotta cheese, egg, parmesan, 1 cup of mozzarella, ½ teaspoon of salt, and pepper to taste until combined.

3 Set aside.

4 Heat a medium pan over medium heat and melt your butter.

5 Brown your meat, seasoning it with ½ teaspoon of salt and 1 teaspoon of Italian seasoning.

6 Set aside.

7 Heat about 3 cups of water in a large pot.

8 Add your noodles (we love the gluten-free Jovial™ brand) and cook according to package instructions.

9 Mix your marinara sauce into your meat mixture.

10 Prepare a 9 x 13-inch baking dish by spraying the bottom and sides with avocado oil cooking spray.

11 Now, time to layer! First, cover the bottom with your meat and sauce mixture.

12 Add a layer of noodles.

13 Add a layer of the cheese mixture and then repeat adding meat, noodles, and cheese until all has been used.

14 Top with remaining mozzarella and bake for 45 minutes or until the cheese is golden brown.

YIELDS · 6-8 servings

HOMEMADE HAMBURGER HELPER

Macey

Another core memory is my mom making hamburger helper for my dad, brother, and I. I have always loved hamburger helper, and I think that was partly due to my love for meat and cheese and the fact that so many good memories were connected with food in my childhood. Food can be a kind of record of all the places, cultures, and people that have played a part in our lives, and I hope that you gather around your table with your loved ones and that your heart is warmed and your soul is satisfied. The food is just the cherry on top!

PREP TIME · 10 minutes

COOK TIME · 30 minutes

- 2 pounds ground beef
- 2 tablespoons butter
- ½ teaspoon salt
- ½ teaspoon black pepper
- 1 medium Vidalia onion, chopped
- 1½ teaspoons chili powder
- 1½ teaspoons garlic powder
- 1 teaspoon Cajun seasoning

- 3 cups of water (enough to cover your noodles)
- 16 ounces of your favorite noodles
- 2 cups bone broth
- 1½ cups milk
- 1 tablespoon of ketchup
- 2 tablespoons cornstarch
- 3½ cups shredded cheddar cheese

INSTRUCTIONS

1   Heat a medium saucepan over medium heat and melt your butter.

2   Add your ground beef, season with salt and pepper, and brown.

3   Add in onion and cook until translucent (should be about the same amount of time as completing the browning of your meat).

4   Season your meat with chili powder, garlic powder, and Cajun seasoning.

5   Heat 3 cups of water in a large pot over medium-high heat.

6   Cook noodles according to package instructions.

7   We love to use conchiglie pasta; they look like conch shells.

8   Drain, rinse with cold water, add back to the large pot, and set aside.

9   Dump your meat into your large pot with your noodles.

10   Add your bone broth, milk, ketchup, cornstarch, and cheddar cheese to your pot.

11   Stir until combined and the cheese is melted.

YIELDS · 4-6 servings

BACON WRAPPED BAKED CHICKEN

I created this recipe one evening with my friend, Elle, when both of our husbands were working night shift at the local car factory. Elle and I spent many fun nights with my son, Jasper, in my kitchen cooking up yummy recipes, many of the ones featured in this cookbook. When I asked her what recipes she thought I should include, this one was at the top of her list! Sometimes, baked chicken breast can be extremely dry and unappealing, but this recipe produces moist chicken every single time!

PREP TIME · 10 minutes

COOK TIME · 30 minutes

- 4 medium sized chicken breasts
- 12 strips of bacon, divided
- 1 tablespoon brown sugar
- 1½ teaspoons paprika
- 1 teaspoon dried oregano
- 1 teaspoon seasoning salt
- ½ teaspoon garlic powder
- ½ teaspoon onion powder
- ¼ teaspoon black pepper
- 1 teaspoon chili powder
- 4 tablespoons butter, melted
- 1 teaspoon lemon juice

INSTRUCTIONS

1. Preheat your oven to 425 degrees.
2. Line a large baking sheet with parchment paper.
3. Mix together the brown sugar and seasonings in a small bowl and set aside.
4. Combine the butter and lemon juice.
5. Place your chicken breasts on the baking sheet and brush each with the butter and lemon juice mixture.
6. Wrap each chicken breast with 3 strips of bacon.
7. Season both sides of each chicken breast with the brown sugar and spice mixture.
8. Place in the oven and bake at 425 degrees for 16 to 18 minutes or until chicken and bacon are both cooked.
9. Serve with a side of your favorite vegetables or with rice!

YIELDS · 4 servings

CHICKEN AND DUMPLINGS

Karen

Without a doubt, this is my favorite dish my mother ever made. She made it for me on my birthday right up until she passed away at the age of 87. Now, when I make it for my own family, I miss her every time it's simmering on my stove.

PREP TIME · 20 minutes

COOK TIME · 35-40 minutes

- 6 tablespoons butter
- 1 cup minced onion
- 3 tablespoons all-purpose flour
- 1 can (12 oz.) can evaporated milk
- 32 ounces chicken broth
- 4 cups chopped, cooked chicken
- 2 teaspoons black pepper

- 1 teaspoons salt
- 2 cups all-purpose flour
- 1 tablespoon plus 1 teaspoon, baking powder
- ½ teaspoon black pepper
- 1 teaspoon salt
- ¾ cup half-and-half
- 4 tablespoons butter, melted

INSTRUCTIONS

1 In a Dutch oven or large soup pot, melt butter over medium heat.

2 Add onion and cook for 5 minutes.

3 Add 3 tablespoons of flour, stirring well and cook for 2 minutes.

4 Add evaporated milk and chicken broth.

5 Bring to a low boil and add chicken, pepper, and salt.

6 Simmer over medium-low heat, uncovered, for 10 to 15 minutes.

7 While the pot is simmering, in a large bowl, mix 2 cups flour, baking powder, pepper, and salt.

8 Slowly add half-and-half and melted butter, stirring until a soft ball of dough forms.

9 Then, using a large spoon, scoop dough and drop in 2-inch heaps into the simmering soup, leaving a little space in between each one.

10 Once all dumplings are in the pot, press down on them lightly so the soup moistens them on top.

11 Place the lid on your pot and reduce heat to a very low simmer.

12 Cook for 15 minutes.

13 Cut through one dumpling to make sure they are cooked all the way through.

14 If not, cover the pot again and cook for 5 more minutes.

YIELDS · 6 servings

SLOW COOKER HONEY MUSTARD PORK CHOPS

Karen

When my kids—especially my two sons—were teenagers, they would eat anything with honey mustard on it. These sweet and tangy pork chops fall apart because they are so tender. Serve them with rice or mashed red skinned potatoes.

PREP TIME · 5 minutes

COOK TIME · 4 hours on high or 7-8 hours on low

- 1½ pounds thin, boneless pork chops (about 6 to 8 pork chops)
- ½ cup whole grain mustard (may use regular or Dijon mustard too)
- 3 tablespoons honey
- 2 tablespoons brown sugar
- 1 teaspoon fresh minced garlic
- 1 teaspoon onion powder
- 1 cup chicken broth
- ½ teaspoon pepper
- 2 tablespoons cornstarch plus 3½ tablespoons very cold water
- Cooking spray

INSTRUCTIONS

1   Spray inside of the slow cooker with cooking spray.

2   Place chops in the slow cooker.

3   In a bowl, combine remaining ingredients, except for the cornstarch and water, and pour over the pork chops.

4   Cover and cook on high for 4 hours or on low for 7 to 8 hours.

5   Mix the cornstarch with the cold water and add it to the slow cooker, stirring well.

6   Put the lid back on and let the sauce thicken up for about 10 to 15 minutes longer, then serve.

YIELDS · 6-8 servings

SOUTHERN SHRIMP AND GRITS WITH GRAVY

Macey

Shrimp and grits was one of the entrees at our wedding. The ladies of Lumber City Baptist Church, my home church for 26 years, really outdid themselves! The food was truly phenomenal per usual, and my husband has requested this dish countless times since we were married five years ago. I asked for the recipe right after I moved to Michigan, and they obliged. I've tweaked it to fit mine and my family's preferences, and we captured the flavor perfectly. If you're looking for a truly Southern dish, this would be it!

PREP TIME · 10 minutes

COOK TIME · 45 minutes

- 2 cups bone broth
- 1½ cups whole milk
- ⅓ cup butter
- 1 teaspoon salt
- ½ teaspoon pepper
- ½ teaspoon hot sauce
- 1 cup uncooked, old-fashioned grits
- 1 cup shredded cheddar cheese
- ½ cup cream cheese
- 1 pound shrimp, peeled and deveined
- 1 teaspoon Cajun seasoning
- 2 tablespoons butter
- ½ Vidalia onion, chopped
- ½ bell pepper, finely chopped
- 2 tablespoons cornstarch
- 1 cup heavy cream
- 1 cup half-and-half
- 8 strips of bacon, cooked and chopped

INSTRUCTIONS

1 In a large pot, bring bone broth, milk, butter, salt, pepper, and hot sauce to a boil.

2 Slowly stir in grits.

3 Cover and cook for 15 to 20 minutes or until grits are done (they should thicken up).

4 Stir in cheddar cheese and cream cheese until melted.

5 Set aside and keep warm.

6 Season your shrimp with Cajun seasoning.

7 In a large skillet, melt the butter over medium heat.

8 Cook shrimp until pink, about 1 to 2 minutes on each side.

9 Set aside and keep warm.

10 Next, add the onion and bell pepper to the skillet, cooking until the onion is translucent and the bell pepper is tender, about 7 to 10 minutes.

11 Add 2 tablespoons of cornstarch to the mixture followed by the heavy cream and half-and-half.

12 Whisk to combine constantly stirring until the gravy has thickened.

13 Add your bacon to the gravy.

14 Put grits in your bowl followed by a generous helping of shrimp.

15 Top off your entree with gravy and enjoy!

YIELDS · 4-6 servings

DELICIOUS PRESSURE COOKER PULLED PORK

Macey

Another amazing pressure cooker recipe! When you use meat from pigs that were raised organically and on pasture, the taste is unmatched! That's how we raise our pigs at The Farm on Federal. It's worth every extra penny and all the hard work to raise meat that we know has had a wonderful life in the outdoors and the sunshine with no antibiotics!

PREP TIME · 30 minutes

COOK TIME · 1 hour 55 minutes

- 1 pork butt shoulder (7 pounds)
- 2 tablespoons olive oil
- 2 tablespoons favorite pork butt rub
- 1 cup Vidalia onion, chopped
- 1 teaspoon minced garlic
- 1 cup bone broth, divided
- 1 cup Vidalia onion BBQ sauce
- 1 cup Vidalia onion honey mustard
- ¼ cup apple cider vinegar
- ¼ cup pineapple juice

INSTRUCTIONS

1   Prepare your pork butt shoulder by cutting it into manageable sections so that it can all fit into your pressure cooker.

2   Liberally season your pork butt shoulder pieces with pork butt rub.

3   Start with 2 tablespoons and add more if needed.

4   Turn your pressure cooker to the sauté setting.

5   Allow it to warm and then add your olive oil.

6   Brown each pork butt shoulder section, about 1 to 2 minutes per side.

7   When done, set each section aside.

8   Add ½ cup of bone broth to your pressure cooker to deglaze it.

9   Scrape the bottom with a wooden spoon.

10   Turn your pressure cooker off and add your onion, allowing it to cook for about 1 minute.

11   Add the rest of your bone broth and the minced garlic.

12   Add your pork butt shoulder sections to the pressure cooker.

13   Add BBQ sauce, honey mustard, apple cider vinegar, and pineapple juice, pouring on top of your pork butt.

14   Set the venting knob to the sealing position.

15   Pressure cook on high for 90 minutes.

16   Allow it to naturally release, about 25 additional minutes.

17   Open your pressure cooker and shred your meat with a fork.

18   Eat as is or make a pulled pork sandwich with fresh sourdough sandwich bread!

YIELDS · 4-6 servings

BREADS, ROLLS, MUFFINS & MORE!

"The smell of good bread baking, like the sound of lightly flowing water, is indescribable in its evocation of innocence and delight."

— M.F.K. FISHER

Bread is so therapeutic. Whether making it, smelling it baking, or happily eating it, something about bread soothes the soul. Here you will discover creative recipes for breads, rolls, muffins, and more. Consider making some extras to freeze for future use.

MAMMIE'S SOUTHERN CORNBREAD

Macey

Mammie was my grandpa's mom. She lived through the Great Depression and were sharecroppers as well. Mammie knew what it meant to go without, but she also knew how to make what she did have go a long way. Making cornbread this way and putting it in soup made your food last longer and made you full faster! Not only that, but it is delicious as well!

PREP TIME · 5 minutes

COOK TIME · 20 minutes

- 2 cups fresh ground cornmeal
- 1 teaspoon baking powder (you do not need this if you have self-rising cornmeal)
- 1 teaspoon salt
- 1 to 2 cups buttermilk
- 12 to 16 tablespoons butter, to grease the pan

INSTRUCTIONS

1   In a medium bowl, mix dry ingredients together.

2   Slowly add buttermilk until you reach the desired consistency similar to cake batter.

3   Batter should easily pour from a spoon, but should not be too soupy.

4   Heat 2 tablespoons of butter in a cast iron pan over medium heat.

5   When the pan is hot enough, spoon 4 tablespoons of cornbread mixture into your pan.

6   Cook until golden brown on one side (about 5 minutes), pick up cornbread with your spatula, put 1 tablespoon of butter in the pan, and flip the cornbread.

7   Cook until golden brown on the other side, about 5 minutes.

8   Repeat until all of the mixture has been used.

YIELDS · 4-6 servings

GRANDMA KIT'S NORTHERN CORNBREAD

Karen

When my kids were little, my daughter, Kenna, often asked me to make this dish. We called it Johnny cake, after the treat author Laura Ingalls Wilder mentioned in her books in the Little House *series. Kenna and her baby brothers loved it for breakfast with butter on top and drizzled with maple syrup. Now I–Grandma Kit–can make it for my Grandson, Jasper. NOTE: This recipe can also be used in Granny Brewer's Turkey Dressing recipe—where the Midwest and South unite to make a classic holiday side dish.*

PREP TIME · 20 minutes
COOK TIME · 20 minutes

- 1 cup yellow cornmeal
- 1 cup all-purpose flour
- ½ cup sugar
- 2 teaspoons baking powder
- 1 teaspoon salt
- ½ teaspoon baking soda
- ¾ cup sour cream

- ½ cup full-fat buttermilk (not reduced fat)
- 2 large eggs, beaten
- 3 tablespoons melted butter, cooled slightly
- 2 tablespoons olive oil
- Cooking spray
- 1 round cake pan (8-inch)

INSTRUCTIONS

1 Preheat the oven to 400 degrees.

2 In a large bowl, whisk together cornmeal, flour, sugar, baking powder, salt, and baking soda.

3 In a separate medium bowl, stir together sour cream, buttermilk, eggs, melted butter, and olive oil.

4 Spoon the wet ingredients into the dry ingredients.

5 Fold just until combined.

6 Spray the pan with cooking spray and pour batter into the pan.

7 Bake for 18 to 22 minutes or until a toothpick inserted comes out clean.

8 Remove and let cool until just slightly.

9 Warm leftovers before serving.

YIELDS · 4-6 servings

PARKER HOUSE ROLLS

Karen

These are hands down the best dinner rolls I have ever made. They won me the blue-ribbon rosette at the Clinton County Fair in Michigan when I was a stay-at-home mom of three young kids. My mother said she remembers eating Parker House rolls when she was a little girl, and I loved making these for holiday get-togethers at her house.

PREP TIME · 2 hours and 15 minutes, including rise time
COOK TIME · 15-20 minutes

- 5 tablespoons melted butter, slightly cooled
- ⅓ cup sugar
- 1 teaspoon salt
- 1 large egg, lightly beaten
- 1½ cups very warm water (110 to 115 degrees Fahrenheit)
- 1 packet yeast
- 4 cups bread flour (not all-purpose flour)
- Additional butter for brushing on top once done
- 1 cookie or biscuit cutter (3-inch) or a regular size canning jar ring

INSTRUCTIONS

1. Mix melted butter, sugar, salt, egg, and warm water in a large bowl.
2. Sprinkle yeast on top and mix in. Let proof for 5 minutes.
3. Then, add flour, mixing well. The dough will be very moist.
4. Cover the bowl with plastic wrap that has been sprayed with cooking spray to prevent sticking, and let rise until doubled, about 45 minutes.
5. Pour the dough onto a well-floured counter.
6. Using a floured rolling pin, roll out to ½ inch thickness.
7. Cut into rounds with a 3-inch cookie cutter.
8. Fold each round in half so they look like little taco shells and place them in three long rows, side-by-side with the folded ends pointing down, in a greased 9 x 13-inch pan. (There will be about 36 little taco shell-shaped rounds of dough in all. Lay them out in pairs in three long rows.)
9. Cover with plastic wrap that has been sprayed with cooking spray to prevent sticking.
10. Let rise for 30 minutes.
11. While they are rising, preheat the oven to 350 degrees.
12. Uncover and bake for 15 to 20 minutes until lightly golden brown.
13. Brush tops with melted butter and cool.

YIELDS · About 18 pull-apart rolls

BUTTERMILK HONEY-OAT BREAD

Karen

I love kneading bread and watching it rise—not to mention smelling it bake! The whole process slows me down and relaxes me. Whip up a batch of this and watch it disappear. Great for sandwiches or morning toast.

PREP TIME · About 3 hours, including rise time
COOK TIME · 35-40 minutes

- 1 cup old-fashioned oats (not quick oats or instant)
- 4 tablespoons butter
- 2 cups full-fat buttermilk (not reduced-fat)
- ½ cup very warm water (110 to 115 degrees Fahrenheit)
- ½ cup honey
- 1½ teaspoons salt
- 2 packages instant yeast (or 4½ teaspoons bulk)
- 2½ cups whole wheat flour
- 2 cups bread flour (or slightly more)
- 1 tablespoon melted butter
- 1 tablespoon honey
- 2 tablespoons dry oatmeal
- 2 loaf pans (9-inch)

Love each other with genuine affection, and take delight in honoring each other.

ROMANS 12:10 (NLT)

INSTRUCTIONS

1 In a large bowl, place oats and butter.

2 In a medium saucepan, heat buttermilk just until it simmers over low heat.

3 Be careful it does not get too warm and curdle.

4 Pour milk over oats and butter and stir well.

5 Let sit for an hour on the counter, stirring occasionally.

6 Add warm water, honey, salt, and yeast to the bowl and mix well.

7 Add the whole wheat flour in, about 1 cup at a time, mixing well.

8 Then, add just enough of the bread flour to make a soft dough that is not stiff but also not too sticky.

9 Mix well with your hands until a ball of dough forms.

10 On a lightly floured counter, knead dough for 10 minutes until smooth and elastic. (May also use a stand mixer with the dough hook attachment.)

11 Place the dough in an oiled bowl.

12 Cover with a thin dish towel and place in a warm place to rise until doubled, about 1 hour. (Time will depend on the temperature and humidity of the kitchen.) Punch down and divide in half.

13 Shape into 2 loaves.

14 Place in 2 buttered 9-inch loaf pans and preheat the oven to 350 degrees.

15 Cover with a thin dish towel and let rise in a warm place for about 45 to 60 minutes or until it is just about an inch above the top of the pan.

16 Bake at 350 degrees for 30 to 40 minutes until lightly golden.

17 When the bread is done, brush each loaf with melted butter.

18 Warm the tablespoon of honey in the microwave for a few seconds so it will easily spread.

19 Spread on top of the loaf, covering it completely.

20 Sprinkle loaves with 2 tablespoons of dry oatmeal.

21 Let cool before slicing.

YIELDS · Two loaves of 10-12 slices

MULTIGRAIN BREAD

Karen

This recipe makes two loaves of the softest multigrain bread ever! Fabulous when served with butter and whipped honey. Keep one loaf for yourself and give another one away. Add a handwritten tag that reads, "They broke bread in their homes and ate together with glad and sincere hearts." Acts 2:46

PREP TIME · 4 hours, 20 minutes, including rise time
COOK TIME · 35-40 minutes

- 2 packages yeast
- 5 tablespoons honey, divided
- 2¼ cup very warm water, divided (about 110 degrees Fahrenheit)
- ½ cup 7 grain hot cereal dry mix (I use Bob's Red Mill)
- 1½ cups old fashioned oatmeal
- 1 cup whole wheat flour, divided
- ½ cup flaxseeds
- 4 cups bread flour, divided
- 1 tablespoon salt
- ½ cup melted salted butter
- 2 tablespoons more melted butter, for brushing on top when done
- 2 loaf pans (9-inch)

INSTRUCTIONS

1   In a large bowl, mix the yeast, 1 tablespoon honey, and ¼ cup warm water.

2   Let bubble for 5 to 10 minutes.

3   Add remaining 2 cups of warm water, the remaining honey, seven grain cereal, oatmeal, ½ cup of the whole wheat flour, flaxseeds, 1 cup of bread flour, stirring until well mixed.

4   Cover with a thin kitchen towel and set in a warm place to rise for about 45 to 60 minutes.

5   Stir the mixture down and add the salt and ½ cup melted butter.

6   Mix in the remaining whole wheat flour and enough of the remaining bread flour to make an elastic dough.

7   Knead for 10 minutes, until smooth and elastic.

8   Place in a large, oiled bowl.

9   Cover bowl with a thin kitchen towel and place in a warm spot to rise until doubled, about 1½ hours.

10 Punch down dough and let rest 15 minutes.

11 Form into 2 loaves and place in greased 9-inch loaf pans.

12 Cover loosely with a thin kitchen towel.

13 Let rise for 1 hour or about an inch above the top of the pan.

14 While rising, preheat the oven to 375 degrees.

15 Bake loaves for 35-40 minutes or until light golden brown.

16 Cover loosely with aluminum foil for the last 15 minutes if they start to brown too quickly.

17 Loaves will sound hollow when tapped if they are done.

18 Remove and brush with melted butter.

19 Let cool in the pans for 20 minutes and then remove.

20 Place on a wire rack to finish cooling.

YIELDS · 2 loaves of 10-12 slices

BUTTERY SOFT PARMESAN-HERBED BREADSTICKS

Karen

These are ah-mazing! So soft, buttery, and perfectly seasoned. Serve with any Italian dish, soup, or on pizza night with some marinara or ranch dipping sauce. Bet you can't eat just one.

PREP TIME · 25 minutes plus about 2 ½ hours rise time

COOK TIME · 10-12 minutes

Dough

- 1 cup + 2 tablespoons very warm water (110 to 115 degrees Fahrenheit)
- 1 packet instant yeast
- 2 tablespoons sugar
- 4 tablespoons butter, melted
- 1 teaspoon salt
- 3 cups bread flour (or a bit more)

Topping

- 3 tablespoons unsalted butter, melted
- ½ teaspoon salt
- ½ teaspoon garlic powder
- ½ teaspoon Italian seasoning (see our recipe for *Italian Seasoning Mix* on page 229)
- ¼ cup grated Parmesan cheese

1 In a large bowl, combine all ingredients for dough except flour.

2 Gradually stir in flour by hand until a soft, slightly stiff dough forms, adding more flour if necessary just 1 tablespoon at a time. (You can also use a stand mixer with a dough hook, if desired.) Knead dough for 10 minutes, or until smooth and elastic.

3 Place dough in an oiled bowl and cover with a thin kitchen towel.

4 Let rise until doubled in size, about 1½ hours or longer depending on the temperature.

5 Punch down dough and divide into 12 pieces.

6 Roll each piece of dough into a 7-inch breadstick.

7 Place on a parchment-lined baking sheet or one that has been sprayed with cooking spray.

8 Cover lightly with a thin kitchen towel and let rise until doubled in size, about 45 minutes to 1 hour.

9 Preheat the oven to 400 degrees.

10 Bake breadsticks for about 10 to 12 minutes, or until light golden brown.

11 In a small bowl, combine melted butter, salt, garlic powder, and Italian seasonings.

12 Remove breadsticks from the oven and immediately brush with butter mixture and sprinkle with Parmesan cheese.

13 Serve warm.

YIELDS · 12 breadsticks

CITRUS POPPYSEED MUFFINS WITH VANILLA-ALMOND GLAZE

Karen

There is just something that brings a smile to your face when you are eating a muffin. These bright and citrusy ones are oh-so-moist! Serve with a cup of hot tea for a lovely afternoon pick-me-up.

PREP TIME · 20 minutes
COOK TIME · 15-20 minutes

- 2¼ cups all-purpose flour, spooned in measuring cup lightly and leveled
- ¾ cup granulated sugar
- ½ teaspoon salt
- 2 teaspoons baking powder
- ¼ teaspoon baking soda
- 2 tablespoons poppy seeds
- 2 large eggs, room temperature
- ½ cup extra-virgin olive oil
- ½ cup buttermilk, room temperature
- ¼ cup lemon juice
- ½ teaspoon real orange extract
- 1 tablespoon lemon zest

Vanilla-Almond Glaze

- ⅔ cup powdered sugar, or more if too thin
- 3 tablespoons half-and-half (or whole milk)
- ⅛ teaspoon real vanilla extract
- ⅛ teaspoon real almond extract

Hospitality Hack

When preparing a dish to serve your company that calls for lemon juice, zap lemons in the microwave for 10 seconds. Then, roll them around on the counter, pressing down with the palm of your hand. This will yield a lot more juice than just trying to juice them when they are still cold from the refrigerator.

1 Preheat the oven to 375 degrees.

2 In a large bowl, combine the flour, sugar, salt, baking powder, baking soda, and poppy seeds.

3 In a medium bowl, whisk the eggs with vegetable oil, buttermilk, lemon juice, orange extract, and lemon zest.

4 Spoon the wet ingredients into the dry ingredients just until moistened.

5 Do not over-mix.

6 Place the batter into 12-14 lined muffin cups and bake for 15 to 20 minutes until a toothpick inserted comes out clean.

7 Remove from the oven and cool in the pan for 10 minutes before placing muffins on a cooling rack.

8 In a small bowl, whisk together the powdered sugar, half-and-half, vanilla extract, and almond extract to make a pourable glaze.

9 If it is too thin, add more sugar.

10 Drizzle the glaze on top of the muffins.

YIELDS · 12-14 muffins

CRANBERRY-ORANGE SCONES

Karen

Trust me—these scones are as good as the ones at the fancy bakery. If fresh cranberries aren't in season, you may use dried ones instead. You can also substitute fresh blueberries for the cranberries to add a different twist.

PREP TIME · 15 minutes
COOK TIME · 15-17 minutes

- ½ cup sugar
- 1 tablespoon orange zest
- 2¼ cups all-purpose flour
- 1 tablespoon baking powder
- ⅓ teaspoon cream of tartar
- ½ teaspoon salt
- ¾ teaspoon cinnamon
- ½ cup unsalted cold butter, cut into pieces
- 1 large egg
- 3 tablespoons sour cream
- 3 tablespoons whipping cream or half-and-half, plus more for brushing on top
- 2 tablespoons orange juice
- ¾ teaspoon vanilla extract
- 1 cup fresh cranberries

Nutmeg Glaze

- 3 tablespoons butter, melted
- ½ teaspoon vanilla extract
- 2 tablespoons half-and-half
- ¼ teaspoon ground nutmeg
- 1¼ cups powdered sugar (or more)

INSTRUCTIONS

1 Preheat the oven to 400 degrees and line a large baking sheet with parchment paper or spray with baking spray.

2 In a large bowl, mix sugar, orange zest, flour, baking powder, cream of tartar, salt, and cinnamon until well combined.

3 Using a pastry cutter, cut in cold butter until the dough resembles coarse crumbs.

4 Whisk egg, sour cream, whipping cream, orange juice, and vanilla extract together.

5 Then, mix the wet ingredients with the dry ingredients, mixing until just combined.

6 Gently fold in the cranberries.

7 Turn dough out onto a floured counter and pat into a circle about 1 inch thick.

8 Using a sharp knife, cut the dough into 8 triangles.

9 Place the scones on the baking sheet two inches apart.

10 Brush the tops with whipping cream.

11 Bake for 15 to 17 minutes, until lightly golden.

12 Let cool slightly while making the glaze.

13 Blend the melted butter, vanilla extract, and half-and-half in a small bowl.

14 Whisk in nutmeg and sugar until it reaches a pouring consistency.

15 Drizzle the glaze over the cooled scones.

YIELDS · 8 scones

CRUMB TOP APPLE-WALNUT MUFFINS

Karen

These are the perfect contrasting combo of a moist and tart inside and a sweet and crunchy top. Whip up a batch for someone who needs a little cheering or give some to your favorite teacher. Add a hand-written tag that says, "Keep me as the apple of your eye; hide me in the shadow of your wings." Psalm 17:8

PREP TIME · 15 minutes
COOK TIME · 18-22 minutes

- 2 cups all-purpose flour
- ¾ cup granulated sugar
- 1½ teaspoon baking powder
- ½ teaspoon baking soda
- ¼ teaspoon salt
- ½ teaspoon ground cinnamon
- ¼ teaspoon ground nutmeg
- ¼ teaspoon ground ginger
- ¼ teaspoon ground allspice (or 1¼ teaspoons pumpkin pie spice)
- 1 cup buttermilk (not reduced fat)
- 1 large egg, lightly beaten
- ¼ cup plus 2 tablespoons vegetable oil
- 1 teaspoon pure vanilla extract
- 2 cups peeled, chopped cooking apples, such as Granny Smith, Golden Delicious or Spy
- ¾ cup walnuts, coarsely chopped

Crumb Topping

- 6 tablespoons butter, melted and slightly cooled
- 1½ cup all-purpose flour
- ⅓ cup packed light brown sugar
- ⅓ cup granulated sugar
- 1¼ teaspoon cinnamon
- ½ teaspoon salt

INSTRUCTIONS

1 Preheat the oven to 400 degrees.

2 Line a 12-count muffin pan with liners or spray with a baking spray that is a combination of flour and oil, such as Baker's Joy.

3 In a large bowl, combine dry ingredients.

4 In a medium bowl, combine wet ingredients.

5 Make a well in the center of the dry ingredients and pour in the wet ingredients, mixing just until moistened.

6 Fold in apples and walnuts.

7 Spoon into muffin tins.

8 In a small bowl, mix dry ingredients for crumb topping.

9 Add melted and cooled butter and stir until crumbly.

10 Sprinkle crumb topping evenly over muffins and press down lightly.

11 Bake muffins at 400 degrees for 8 minutes.

12 Lower the temperature to 375 degrees and continue baking muffins for another 12 to 14 minutes until a toothpick inserted comes out clean.

13 Cool slightly before serving.

YIELDS · 12 muffins

Do not withhold good from those who deserve it when it's in your power to help them.

PROVERBS 3:27 (NLT)

CAPPUCCINO MUFFINS WITH CREAM CHEESE ESPRESSO SPREAD

Karen

Years ago, my friend Carmen and I held a monthly get-together for women called Mug & Muffin. *Women brought a coffee mug, and we provided muffins and hot drinks. We took turns having someone teach from an area of expertise such as decorating, cooking, summer ideas for children, menu planning, DIY furniture painting, daily personal Bible study ideas, or getting organized. I often made these muffins, and they were always a hit.*

PREP TIME · 20 minutes
COOK TIME · 15-18 minutes

Espresso Spread

- 4 ounces cream cheese, cubed
- 2 tablespoons powdered sugar
- ½ teaspoon instant coffee granules
- ¾ teaspoon vanilla extract
- ⅓ cup mini semi-sweet chocolate chips

Muffins

- 2 cups all-purpose flour
- ¾ cup sugar
- 2½ teaspoons baking powder
- 1¼ teaspoons ground cinnamon
- ½ teaspoon salt
- 2½ tablespoons instant coffee granules
- 1 cup whole milk
- ½ cup butter, melted, and slightly cooled
- 1¼ teaspoons vanilla extract
- 1 egg, well beaten
- 1 cup mini semi-sweet chocolate chips

1   Preheat oven to 375 degrees.

2   In a food processor, combine the ingredients for the espresso spread until well blended.

3   Cover and refrigerate until serving.

4   In a medium bowl, stir together the flour, sugar, baking powder, cinnamon, and salt.

5   In another medium bowl, dissolve the instant coffee granules in the milk and then add the butter, vanilla, and egg.

6   Combine the wet and dry ingredients, mixing just until moistened.

7   Gently fold in the chocolate chips.

8   Place batter in 12 to 14 paper lined muffin cups.

9   Bake at 375 degrees for 15 to 18 minutes or until a toothpick inserted comes out clean.

10   Cool for 10 minutes before removing from the pan.

11   Serve with espresso spread.

YIELDS · 12-14 muffins

GINGERBREAD MUFFINS WITH ORANGE GLAZE

Karen

These aromatic and moist muffins, have a delicious bright, citrus glaze. Don't limit yourself to only making these at the holidays. They are a scrumptious treat anytime of the year. A mini-vacation during an afternoon break in your day when paired with a steaming cup of coffee or tea.

PREP TIME · 20 minutes
COOK TIME · 17-21 minutes

- ½ cup butter
- ¾ cup unsulphured molasses (I use Grandma's original brand)
- 2⅔ cups unbleached all-purpose flour (spooned lightly in the cup)
- 1¾ teaspoons baking soda
- ¼ teaspoon salt
- 1½ teaspoons ground cinnamon
- 1¾ teaspoons ground ginger
- ½ teaspoon ground cloves
- ½ teaspoon ground allspice
- ¼ teaspoon ground nutmeg
- ½ cup brown sugar, packed
- 1 large egg, at room temperature
- ½ cup sour cream, at room temperature
- ½ cup buttermilk or whole milk, at room temperature

Orange Glaze

- 1 cup (or more) powdered sugar
- 2 tablespoons orange juice
- ¼ teaspoon real orange extract
- 1 tablespoon half-and-half

1   Preheat the oven to 425 degrees.

2   Spray a muffin tin with baking spray that has both oil and flour in it, such as Baker's Joy, or line tin with muffin liners.

3   In a medium saucepan over low heat, melt the butter with the molasses, stirring well.

4   Let cool.

5   In a large bowl, stir together the flour, baking soda, salt, and all spices.

6   In a medium bowl, stir the brown sugar, egg, sour cream, and buttermilk until well combined.

7   Pour wet ingredients into dry ingredients and whisk just until combined.

8   Spoon batter into muffin cups until a little over ¾ full.

9   Bake at 425 degrees for 7 minutes and then decrease the oven temperature to 350 degrees and continue to bake for 10 to 14 minutes until a toothpick inserted comes out clean.

10 Remove from the oven and let cool for 15 minutes in the pan before removing.

11 To make the glaze, mix all the ingredients together in a medium bowl until it is a slightly thick but pourable consistency.

12 Drizzle on top of muffins.

YIELDS · 12 muffins

DESSERTS & SWEETS

I can't believe I got this far without realizing I can have dessert every night.

— HARRY POTTER

The closing curtain. The final hurrah. The perfect ending. That
is what dessert dishes are! Enjoy some of our family's favorite
treats to eat, as well as to serve to others. These are sure to button
up your meals in a perfect, shimmery-sweet bow.

DOUBLE-DUTCH MOCHA BROWNIES

Who doesn't love the winning combination of chocolate and coffee? These mocha brownies are a chewy delight full of bursts of semi-sweet chocolate in every bite. They will have you skipping for joy! (Get it? Double Dutch=Skipping?)

PREP TIME · 25 minutes
COOK TIME · 18-23 minutes

- 2 tablespoons hot tap water
- 1½ tablespoons instant coffee granules
- ½ cup butter, melted
- 2 large eggs, room temperature
- 1 cup plus 2 tablespoons granulated sugar
- 1½ teaspoons vanilla extract

- ¾ cup all-purpose flour
- ½ cup powdered sugar
- ¾ cup Dutch-process cocoa powder
- ½ teaspoon salt
- 1 cup semi-sweet chocolate chips
- Confectioner's sugar for dusting

INSTRUCTIONS

1   Preheat the oven to 350 degrees.

2   Grease and flour an 8-inch square baking pan or spray with a baking spray that includes both oil and flour, such as Baker's Joy.

3   In a large mixing bowl, add hot water and instant coffee granules.

4   Add butter, eggs, granulated sugar, and vanilla.

5   In a medium bowl, combine the flour, powdered sugar, cocoa powder, and salt.

6   Add the flour mixture to the butter mixture just until combined.

7   Gently fold in the chocolate chips.

8   Pour the batter into the prepared pan.

9   Bake for 18 to 23 minutes.

10 Brownies are done when an inserted toothpick is covered with some clinging crumbs but not moist batter.

11 Cool, dust with powdered sugar, and cut into squares.

12 Serve at room temperature.

13 Store in a covered container (if they last that long!)

YIELDS · 9 brownies

MICHIGAN DRIED CHERRY-CASHEW COOKIES

Another blue-ribbon rosette winning recipe at my local county fair. These cookies were awarded the first rosette I ever won! I love using products from Michigan and we are famous for our abundant crops of cherries, both tart and dark, sweet. These use dried tart cherries and are a unique treat that always draws rave reviews. They look so pretty too, with half of them dipped in melted white chocolate.

PREP TIME · 15 minutes, plus 4 hours or more to chill dough

COOK TIME · 9-12 minutes

- 1 cup butter, softened
- ¾ cup sugar
- ¾ cup brown sugar, firmly packed
- 2 eggs
- 1 teaspoon vanilla extract
- 2¼ cups all-purpose unbleached flour
- 1 teaspoon baking soda
- 1 teaspoon salt
- 2 cups dried tart Michigan cherries
- 1 cup lightly salted cashew halves and pieces
- 10 ounces white chocolate chips

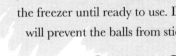

Hospitality Hack

To be ready for unexpected company who might stop by to visit, keep balls of frozen cookie dough in your freezer, ready to be freshly baked into cookies. To do this, mix up your favorite cookie dough. Place balls of cookie dough on a baking sheet in the freezer for at least 8 hours. Remove and place in a plastic freezer bag with a zip closure. Return to the freezer until ready to use. Doing it this way will prevent the balls from sticking together.

INSTRUCTIONS

1   In a medium bowl, cream butter and both sugars together using a hand blender on medium speed.

2   Mix in eggs and vanilla.

3   In a large bowl, mix the flour, baking soda, and salt.

4   Add creamed butter mixture to the dry ingredients, mixing thoroughly.

5   Fold in dried cherries, and cashews.

6   Mix just until blended.

7   Cover the bowl tightly with plastic wrap and let dough chill for at least 4 hours or overnight.

8   Preheat the oven to 375 degrees.

9   Drop chilled dough by heaping tablespoons onto an ungreased cookie sheet.

10   Bake for 9 to 12 minutes or until light golden brown.

11   Cool slightly and transfer to a cooling rack.

12   In a small saucepan over very low heat, melt the white chocolate chips.

13   Dip cookies halfway into the melted chips, covering just half of the cookie.

14   Set on wax paper to harden.

YIELDS · 4 to 4 ½ dozen cookies

GRANDMA GIG'S SALTY TOP OATMEAL COOKIES

Karen

My late stepmother, Mary, was affectionately called Gig. Grandma Gig was a gentle soul who loved to hunt for bargains at garage sales and thrift shops, watch reruns of The Golden Girls, *and play bingo. She also loved cooking and baking for her family and neighbors. My kids always knew Grandma Gig would have some homemade goody for them to snack on when they were at her house. These chewy oatmeal cookies were one of her signature treats. You can add in up to 1 cup chocolate chips, raisins, nuts, or dried cranberries or cherries but we love them just the way she made them—plain and baked with love.*

PREP TIME · 15 minutes, plus 2 hours to chill dough
COOK TIME · 10-13 minutes

- 1 cup all-purpose flour
- ¾ teaspoon baking powder
- ½ teaspoon baking soda
- ¼ teaspoon salt
- ¾ cup real unsalted butter
- 1 cup sugar
- ¼ cup brown sugar, packed
- 1 egg, beaten
- 1 teaspoon pure vanilla extract
- 2½ cup quick-cooking oats (not rolled oats)
- Coarse salt, for topping

INSTRUCTIONS

1. In a medium bowl, combine the flour, baking powder, baking soda, and salt.

2. In a large bowl, using a mixer on medium speed, cream together the butter, sugar, and brown sugar until fluffy.

3. Mix in egg and vanilla, blending well.

4. Blend dry ingredients into the butter mixture just until combined. Do not over mix.

5. Stir in the oats. Cover dough and chill for 2 hours.

6. Preheat the oven to 350 degrees.

7. Using a tablespoon or small cookie scoop, make dough into 2-inch balls, about the size of golf balls.

8. Dip each ball into a small bowl of coarse salt and place on a cookie sheet lined with parchment paper with the salty sides up.

9. Bake for 10 to 13 minutes, or a little longer, just until lightly golden.

10. Cool for 5 to 10 minutes then remove from the pan.

YIELDS · About 3 dozen cookies

PEANUT BUTTER BLONDIES

Karen

These are a nutty twist on a traditional brownie. They are moist, chewy, and flavorful and they also freeze well. If making them, double the recipe so you can cut one pan into squares and freeze them for when unexpected company drops by. Or, mail them to a far-away friend who could use some happy mail.

PREP TIME · 10 minutes

COOK TIME · 40-45 minutes

- 1 cup creamy peanut butter
- 11 tablespoons unsalted butter, softened
- 1 cup brown sugar, packed
- 1 ⅓ cups sugar white granulated
- 2½ teaspoons vanilla
- 4 large eggs
- 2 cups all-purpose flour
- 2¼ teaspoons baking powder
- ¾ teaspoon salt
- Optional: ½ cup chocolate chips

INSTRUCTIONS

1 Preheat the oven to 325 degrees.

2 In a large bowl, blend the peanut butter, butter, sugars, and vanilla.

3 Add in the eggs, one at a time, beating well.

4 In a medium bowl, stir together the flour, baking powder, and salt.

5 Combine the wet and dry ingredients, mixing just until combined.

6 If adding chocolate chips, gently fold them in.

7 Pour batter into a 9 x 13-inch pan that has been sprayed with cooking spray.

8 Bake for 40 to 45 minutes or a tad longer until a toothpick inserted comes out clean.

Hint: If you don't want the edges to be crispy, place strips of foil over about the outer one inch of the pan's sides before baking.

YIELDS · 16 blondies

MEMA'S BANANA PUDDING

Macey

I grew up across the road from my Mema and Papa, my mom's parents. I lived at their house just as much as my own. This is the recipe that my Mema was famous for, and when I see a banana pudding, I always think of her. When I asked my mom for this recipe, I assumed it would be much more in depth and complicated because the taste was always out of this world! Cheers to a truly special and classy lady and an amazing cook to boot! I know she would be so proud of the accomplished person that I am today—her prayers certainly carried me to this point!

PREP TIME · 5 minutes

COOK TIME · 20 minutes

- ¾ cup granulated sugar, divided
- ⅓ cup flour
- ⅛ teaspoon salt
- 3 eggs, separated
- 2 cups milk
- ½ teaspoon vanilla
- 45 vanilla wafers
- 5 ripe bananas, sliced

SOUL SOOTHER

Community is so important for our mental health, as Macey found during the pandemic. When she thinks of community, she thinks of gathering in a living space with a cup of warm coffee and a sweet treat like this one. Community is important to help us through the highs and lows of life and to act as a protective factor when life gets tough. Two people who come to Macey's mind are her very dear friends, Miss Stephanie and Alyssia—a mother-daughter combo who are always there with an encouraging word, a hug, a prayer. We encourage you to find your own community and love them well!

INSTRUCTIONS

1   Mix ½ cup of sugar, flour, and salt in the top of a double boiler.

2   Blend in 3 egg yolks and milk.

3   Cook uncovered over boiling water, stirring constantly for 10 to 12 minutes or until thickened.

4   Remove from heat and stir in vanilla.

5   Add the sliced bananas and vanilla wafers to the pudding mixture, folding in gently until combined.

6   Transfer to an oven-proof 9 x 13-inch casserole dish.

7   In a mixing bowl or with a hand mixer, whip together ¼ cup sugar and the egg whites until stiff peaks form.

8   Spoon this topping on top of your banana pudding.

9   Broil on low until the peaks are slightly brown.

10 Serve immediately on your finest china or a paper plate—just as long as you serve it to family and friends!

YIELDS · One 9 x 13-inch pan

TATA'S MILLION DOLLAR DESSERT

Macey

Tata was a special lady to me. She is my aunt's mom, and she passed away when I was in my 20s. I grew up going to her home with my cousins Dylan and Derek, watching Braves baseball with her and Grandaddy, and rocking in rocking chairs on her front porch overlooking Airport Road. She was famous for her Million Dollar dessert. I'm not sure who named it, but I can vouch for the fact that anyone would pay a million dollars just to eat a piece. Every time we walked through her door, one of the three of us would ask, "Did you make a million dollars today, Tata?"

PREP TIME · 20 minutes
COOK TIME · 20 minutes

- 1 cup all-purpose flour
- ½ cup salted butter
- ½ cup chopped pecans, divided
- 1 package (8 oz.) of cream cheese, softened
- 1 cup powdered sugar

- 1 carton (16 oz.) of Cool Whip™, thawed (extra creamy preferred)
- 2 small packages instant chocolate pudding
- 3½ cups whole milk

INSTRUCTIONS

1 Preheat your oven to 350 degrees.

2 Mix flour and butter until crumbly.

3 Press into a 9 x 13-inch baking dish.

4 Place ¼ cup of the pecans over the dough.

5 Bake for 20 minutes.

6 Let cool.

7 In a stand mixer, mix cream cheese and powdered sugar until incorporated.

8 Then, stir in ½ carton of Cool Whip™, spread mixture over crust.

9 Mix instant pudding and milk.

10 Spread over the cream cheese layer.

11 Top with remaining Cool Whip™ and pecans.

YIELDS · One 9 x 13-inch dessert

BOSTON GRAHAMS

Karen

This recipe was famous at Camp Barakel, a Christian camp all of my children attended in the summer near the thumb of Michigan. (We Michiganders always have our map at our fingertips since our state is shaped like a hand. You know we are the high five of the United States, right?) My boys especially love this dish and sometimes ask for it on their birthdays instead of cake. You can substitute 3 cups of stiffly beaten whipping cream for the non-dairy whipped topping if you prefer.

PREP TIME · 25 minutes, plus 6 hours chilling time

- 3½ cups whole milk
- 2 boxes (3.4 oz.) vanilla instant pudding
- 1 container frozen non-dairy whipped topping, thawed
- 1 box graham crackers
- 3 ounces unsweetened baker's chocolate
- 2 tablespoons light corn syrup
- ¼ cup salted butter
- ¼ cup hot water
- 1 teaspoon vanilla extract
- 4 cups powdered sugar

INSTRUCTIONS

1 In a medium bowl, mix the milk and pudding together using an electric mixer on medium speed until it thickens.

2 Gently fold in the whipped topping.

3 Line the bottom of a 9 x 13-inch pan with a single layer of graham crackers, breaking some if necessary to fill any gaps.

4 Pour half the pudding mixture over the crackers and spread evenly.

5 Top with another layer of graham crackers.

6 Pour the remaining pudding mixture in and then finish with a third layer of crackers.

7 In a medium saucepan over very low heat, heat the chocolate, corn syrup, and butter until the chocolate is melted.

8 Stir in the quarter cup hot water and vanilla, whisking it until smooth.

9 Then, whisk in the powdered sugar until glassy.

10 If it is too thick, add more hot water, maybe a tablespoon or two.

11 Pour the chocolate evenly over the top of the graham cracker layer.

12 Allow to cool for 15 minutes.

13 Seal with foil and refrigerate at least 6 hours or overnight.

YIELDS · 15 servings

AUNT LORAINE'S PEANUT BUTTER FUDGE

Karen

My sister-in-law, Lorraine, is well known in our family for her quick wit, contagious smile, and—most importantly—her famous peanut butter fantasy fudge! My kids just couldn't get enough of this at our family Christmas gatherings when they were young. So light and fluffy. This classic recipe has been around for decades and it makes a great gift for teachers, neighbors, and coworkers.

PREP TIME · 15 minutes

- 3 cups sugar
- ¾ cup butter or margarine
- 1 can (5 oz.) evaporated milk (about ⅔ cup)
- 1 cup creamy peanut butter
- 1 jar (7 oz.) marshmallow creme
- 1 teaspoon vanilla

INSTRUCTIONS

1   Line a 9-inch square pan with foil, extending foil over the sides.

2   In a medium saucepan, bring the sugar, butter, and milk to full rolling boil over medium heat, stirring constantly.

3   Once it boils, cook for exactly 4 minutes, stirring constantly, or until a candy thermometer reaches 234°F.

4   Remove from heat and stir in peanut butter and marshmallow creme until blended.

5   Add vanilla and stir well.

6   Pour into the prepared pan, spreading evenly.

7   Cool completely before cutting into any size squares you wish.

YIELDS · Between 16 and 36 squares, depending on size (We like 'em huge!)

PAPA'S PEANUT BRITTLE

Macey

My Papa was famous for his peanut brittle, and he made it frequently for his friends, particularly at Ocmulgee Christian Academy where my Mema was a teacher and then the principal. He also made it around the holidays and gave it away as Christmas presents, and many times, he made it just because his sweet tooth was acting up.

PREP TIME · 5 minutes

COOK TIME · 20 minutes, plus 3 hours cooling time

- 1 cup maple syrup
- 2 cups granulated sugar
- 2 cups shelled peanuts (or more depending on preference)
- 1 teaspoon baking soda

INSTRUCTIONS

1 Line a large, sided cookie sheet with parchment paper or spray with cooking spray.

2 In a large and deep cast iron pan over medium heat, cook your maple syrup and sugar until it starts a foamy boil.

3 Add peanuts and cook for 20 minutes.

4 A few minutes before your brittle is done, stir in 1 teaspoon of baking soda.

5 My grandpa's directions say, "Stir until it is the color you want." My Papa always cooked it until it was a golden caramel color.

6 Pour onto the prepared cookie sheet and allow to cool, about 3 hours.

7 Break into pieces and enjoy!

YIELDS · 30 servings

Hospitality Hack

This is a great treat to make as party favors for birthday parties or Christmas parties or as an item in a gift basket! It yields a lot but is a simple recipe to follow! Just break the brittle into pieces, wrap in treat bags, attach a cute card with some ribbon, and you've got a delicious, homemade holiday gift!

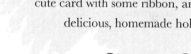

JESSI'S APPLE CIDER DONUTS

Macey

My husband's childhood best friend, Jonny, is married to Jessi. They have three beautiful children, Lincoln, Walter, and Jane. When I moved to Michigan, Jessi and I became friends fast. We bonded over a shared love of the Lord, and we both have been there for each other through the best of times and the worst of times. She's an amazing cook and has adapted her cooking to fit her children's needs. So, this recipe is paleo, dairy-free, and gluten-free, but man, is it packed with flavor! These are my husband's favorite donuts!

PREP TIME · 15 minutes

COOK TIME · 30 minutes

- 1 cup apple cider reduced to about ⅓ cup (see instructions below)
- 2¼ cups blanched almond flour
- ¾ cup arrowroot flour or tapioca
- 1 teaspoon baking soda
- ½ tablespoon apple pie spice
- ½ tablespoon pumpkin pie spice
- 1 teaspoon cinnamon
- ¼ teaspoon salt
- 2 large eggs, at room temperature
- ¾ cup maple sugar or coconut sugar
- 2 tablespoons coconut oil or ghee, melted
- 2 tablespoons almond milk
- 1 teaspoon pure vanilla extract
- Avocado oil cooking spray

Topping

- 2 tablespoons ghee, melted
- ⅓ cup coconut sugar
- ⅓ cup maple sugar
- 1½ teaspoons apple pie spice

INSTRUCTIONS

1 Preheat your oven to 350 degrees.

2 Use a silicone donut pan for this recipe to allow for easy removal.

3 Reduce the apple cider by placing the apple cider in a small saucepan and bringing to a boil.

4 Then, lower the heat to medium and allow it to simmer for about 5 to 8 minutes or until it reduces to about ⅓ cup.

5 Remove from heat and allow it to cool while preparing the rest of the donut batter.

6 In a large mixing bowl, combine the almond flour, arrowroot, baking soda, apple pie spice, pumpkin pie spice, cinnamon, and salt.

7 Set aside.

8 In a separate large bowl, whisk together the eggs, sugar, oil or ghee, almond milk, and vanilla.

9 Whisk in the reduced apple cider.

10 Add the dry ingredients to the wet ingredients and stir until fully combined.

11 Spray your donut pan with avocado oil cooking spray to lightly grease it.

12 Spoon the batter evenly into the wells of the donut pan.

13 Bake for 20 minutes or until set and a toothpick inserted near the middle comes out clean.

14 Remove the pan from the oven and place it on a wire rack to cool for about 5 to 10 minutes.

15 Carefully remove the doughnuts and place them on a wire rack to cool completely.

16 While they cool, make the topping.

17 Mix the coconut and maple sugars and apple pie spice in a small bowl.

18 Brush the cooled donuts with the ghee and either sprinkle with or dip in the sugar mixture.

19 Serve right away or store loosely covered at room temperature for up to 3 days.

YIELDS · 12 donuts

My command is this: Love each other as I have loved you.

JOHN 15:12

MS. DEANN'S BLUEBERRY PINEAPPLE CRUNCH CAKE   *Macey*

I have so many favorite recipes that my mom makes (I'm hoping she's writing a cookbook of her own for my brother, Justin, and me to have one day), but one of my favorites is her blueberry pineapple crunch cake. My dad, brother, and I all enjoy this delightful dessert of hers, and it seems to follow the seasons, as it is delicious on a summer's day with ice cream or in a bowl by itself warming you from the inside out on a cold winter day.

PREP TIME · 15 minutes

COOK TIME · 30 minutes

- 1 can (20 oz.) of crushed pineapple with juice
- 1 can (21 oz.) of blueberry pie filling
- 2½ cups all-purpose flour
- 1½ cups sugar
- 4 teaspoons baking powder
- 1 teaspoon salt
- 4 tablespoons unsalted butter, softened
- ½ cup butter, cold and cubed about ¼ inch thick
- Avocado oil cooking spray

INSTRUCTIONS

1   Preheat your oven to 350 degrees.

2   Spray a 9 x 13-inch baking dish with avocado oil cooking spray.

3   Cover the bottom of the baking dish with the pineapple and juice.

4   Spoon blueberry pie filling on top of your pineapple mixture.

5   In a medium bowl, mix all the dry ingredients with the softened butter.

6   Sprinkle the mixture over the blueberry pie filling, making sure the filling is covered. (You can also use one box of yellow cake mix here if you don't want to make your own dry mix).

7   Then, place pats of cubed butter on top of the dry mixture, making sure to place them evenly.

8   When in doubt, use more butter so that as it melts, it coats the top of the entire dessert.

9   Bake for 30 minutes or until the top is a golden brown.

10   Enjoy warm with your favorite ice cream on top!

YIELDS · One 9 x 13-inch cake

MR. JERRY'S CINNAMON SUGAR TOAST

Macey

My dad made this simple "dessert" all the time during my childhood. I would request it weekly if not daily, and I believe he obliged every time I asked, if not almost every time. It's an easy recipe, and I cannot wait for my dad to make this for my son and to continue the tradition with the next generation.

PREP TIME · 5 minutes
COOK TIME · 5 minutes

- 12 pieces of white bread
- 48 tablespoons of butter, divided
- ½ cup granulated sugar
- 1½ tablespoons cinnamon

INSTRUCTIONS

1. Preheat your oven to broil on low.

2. Line a large baking sheet with parchment paper.

3. Place your pieces of bread on your baking sheet.

Hospitality Hack

You don't have to serve an entire meal to be offering hospitality. Preparing such a feast may be intimidating for you. Simply inviting overs for dessert is still a wonderful way to host others. Serve a sweet dish or two, and brew some coffee or tea. Guests can even balance plates on their laps while you visit in the living room or outdoors.

4. Put 4 tablespoons of butter on each piece of toast.

5. Mix your sugar and cinnamon in a bowl and sprinkle 1 tablespoon of the mixture on each piece of bread.

6. If you have extra "seasoning" leftover, you can go back and add some more to each piece.

7. Put your baking sheet in your oven and broil on low for about 5 minutes or until your toast is golden and your butter is melted.

8. Keep an eye on your bread to make sure it doesn't burn.

9. Take your pan out of the oven, allow to cool for about 1 to 2 minutes, and then eat immediately!

YIELDS · 12 pieces

MOLASSES COOKIE ICE CREAM SANDWICHES

I cannot take credit for this recipe as it was really my husband's idea. He bought me an ice cream maker as a present (I wonder if it was really a present for him!), and he asked me if I could make him an ice cream sandwich using my molasses cookie recipe. I wish you could have seen his face when he bit into this creation for the first time. He was in heaven! You can use your own favorite cookie, homemade or from the grocery store, for this recipe.

PREP TIME · 2 hours

COOK TIME · 30 minutes

- 1½ cups whole milk
- 2 cups heavy cream
- 6 egg yolks
- 2 teaspoons vanilla
- ½ cup honey
- Optional additions: pieces of chocolate, peanut butter, cacao powder, or caramel—as much as is desired!
- 30 Molasses Cookies (see the *Molasses Cookies* recipe on page 194)

Hospitality Hack

For a stress-free get together, hold an old-fashioned ice cream social. You provide the ice cream, either store-bought or hand cranked. Each guest can bring a topping such as hot fudge, caramel, fresh fruit, chopped nuts, coconut, whipped cream, or sprinkles. Don't forget the cherries for the top! Karen's family has done this on June 21, the longest day of the year. It stays late until almost 10 PM in Michigan on that day. Guests can enjoy ice cream and play lawn games and visit until the sun goes down.

INSTRUCTIONS

1. Place all the ice cream ingredients in a blender and blend until smooth.

2. Pour into your ice cream maker and follow the instructions according to your ice cream maker.

3. Usually this takes about 15-25 minutes.

4. When the ice cream is done, take one cookie as your "base," scoop as much ice cream as desired onto the cookie, and top with another cookie.

5. Repeat until all cookies have been used.

6. Place cookie sandwiches on a large baking sheet lined with parchment paper and allow to sit in your freezer for 5 to 10 minutes until frozen.

7. Enjoy!

YIELDS · About 15 ice cream sandwiches

PEANUT BUTTER APPLE CRISP

Karen

If I had a nickel for every time I've made this recipe over the last 25 years, I would be a rich woman! I invented it early on in my marriage because my husband loved the combination of apples and peanut butter. As we had children, they grew to love it too. By the time all of our kids were teenagers, I was constantly making this recipe for their friends to devour. Serve with vanilla ice cream or whipped cream. FABULOUS!!!!!

PREP TIME · 20 minutes
COOK TIME · 25-30 minutes

- 8 to 10 Spy or other tart cooking apples (Granny Smith or Golden Delicious)
- 2 tablespoons lemon juice
- ½ teaspoon salt
- ⅓ cup flour
- 1½ cups sugar

Topping

- ½ cup real butter, softened
- 1½ cups chunky peanut butter
- ½ teaspoon salt
- 1½ cups sugar
- 1 cup flour, or more
- 1½ cups rolled oats (not quick-cooking)

INSTRUCTIONS

1   Preheat the oven to 375 degrees.

2   Spray a 9 x 13-inch pan with cooking spray.

3   Peel and slice enough apples to fill the pan.

4   Sprinkle them with lemon juice and salt.

5   Mix flour and sugar and shake over the top of the apples.

6   Toss gently.

7   In a medium bowl, combine the butter and peanut butter.

8   Add in the rest of the topping ingredients, mixing well. Topping should hold together in clumps when pressed in your fist and not be too sticky. If it is, add a little more flour.

9   Sprinkle topping over the apples and bake at 375 degrees for about 25 to 30 minutes until the apples are tender and the topping is lightly golden.

YIELDS · 12 servings

KERI LYNN'S GEORGIA PECAN PIE

Macey

My sister-in-law, Keri Lynn, is famous for her pecan pie. A native of Georgia, she makes it at my husband's request every time we come home, and you can always find one of her pecan pies at our Thanksgiving or Christmas gatherings. It wouldn't be the holidays without it! Oh, and by the way…in this recipe, "pecan" is pronounced PEE-can, not puh-KAHN. {wink}

PREP TIME · 10 minutes

COOK TIME · 50-55 minutes

- 3 eggs
- 1 cup granulated sugar
- ½ cup butter
- 1 cup maple syrup
- 1 teaspoon vanilla extract
- 1 cup pecans
- 1 pie crust (9-inch). (See *Sourdough Pie Crust* recipe on page 192 or use store bought)

INSTRUCTIONS

1 Preheat your oven to 325 degrees.

2 In a stand mixer, mix your eggs, sugar, and butter together.

3 Then add in your maple syrup, vanilla extract, and your pecans.

4 Add filling to a pie crust.

5 Bake for 50 to 55 minutes or until done.

YIELDS · 8 servings

AUNT PATTY'S PINEAPPLE CHEESECAKE

Karen

I simply loved going to my Aunt Patty and Uncle Lee's house in Milwaukee, Wisconsin. We only went once or twice a year, but I have so many vivid memories of Aunt Patty's gentle voice, her unlimited patience, her sweet-smelling perfume, and her delicious pineapple cheesecake. Today she is the youngest 80-something-year old I know, and I still enjoy spending time with her. Make this sunny cheesecake for someone you love as much as I love my Aunt Patty.

PREP TIME · 30 minutes

COOK TIME · 20 minutes

- 20 whole graham crackers, crushed
- ½ cup butter, melted
- 1¼ cup sugar, divided
- 2 eggs
- 8 ounces cream cheese, softened
- ½ teaspoon vanilla
- 1 can (20 oz.) crushed pineapple with juice
- 4 teaspoons cornstarch

INSTRUCTIONS

1 Preheat the oven to 350 degrees.

2 In a medium bowl, mix together the crushed graham crackers, melted butter, and ½ cup sugar.

3 Press the mixture into a greased 8-inch square pan.

4 In a medium bowl, beat together the eggs, cream cheese, ½ cup sugar, and vanilla.

5 Pour mixture on top of the crust.

6 Bake at 350 degrees for 20 to 25 minutes or until the cheese is solid.

7 Prepare the pineapple topping while the cheesecake is cooking.

8 In a medium saucepan, mix the crushed pineapple with juice together with the ¼ cup sugar and cornstarch.

9 Cook over medium heat until very thick, stirring constantly, about 10 minutes and remove from heat and cool completely.

10 Pour over the cheesecake.

YIELDS · 6-8 servings

RED, WHITE, AND BLUEBERRY PIE

Karen

Need a great recipe to celebrate Memorial Day or Independence Day? How about this: a red, white, and blue-ribbon-winning pie. Top with vanilla ice cream for the color scheme to be complete! (Fresh fruit works best but you can also use thawed, drained frozen fruit too. And don't panic when you see the homemade crust. You can buy a roll-out refrigerated one instead!)

PREP TIME · 15-45 minutes (depending on homemade or store-bought crust)

COOK TIME · 50-60 minutes

Crust

- 3 cups all-purpose flour
- 1 teaspoon salt
- 1 cup lard (or butter, or butter-flavored shortening)
- 1 egg
- 5 tablespoons whole milk or cream
- 1 teaspoon vinegar

Filling

- 2 cups blueberries
- 1½ cups raspberries
- 1½ cups tart cherries, pitted
- 1 cup sugar
- 5 tablespoons flour
- ¼ teaspoon salt
- 1 teaspoon almond extract

Crumb topping:

- ½ cup packed light brown sugar
- 1 cup all-purpose flour
- ½ cup cold unsalted butter

INSTRUCTIONS

1 Preheat the oven to 350 degrees.

2 To make the pie crust, with a pastry blender or large fork, mix flour, salt, lard, and egg until coarse crumbles form.

3 Mix milk and vinegar together and stir in with a light touch until well blended.

4 Combine the wet and dry ingredients to form a ball.

5 On a well-floured surface, roll out half the crust into a circle large enough for your pie pan.

6 Place the crust in a pie pan.

7 Wrap remaining crust in plastic wrap, and place in a freezer bag to freeze for the next time you need a crust, up to 3 months.

8 Mix filling ingredients together well in a medium bowl and place in the crust.

9 In a small bowl, mix brown sugar and flour for the crumb topping.

10 Cut in the butter with a pastry blender or large fork until coarse crumbs form.

11 Sprinkle on top of the pie and press down slightly on any taller peaks so they won't burn.

12 Bake at 350 degrees for 50 to 60 minutes, just until bubbly and the crust is lightly golden.

YIELDS · 8 servings

GRANDMA MARGARET'S GERMAN CHOCOLATE CAKE *Karen*

My mom made the most scrumptious cakes from scratch. She had a tradition of always baking a homemade cake on the first day of school every year. In addition, she would make me white cake with coconut frosting for my birthday or this German chocolate cake for my brother's yearly celebration. One of my favorite childhood memories was smelling a cooling cake on the kitchen counter that had just come out of our avocado green oven. If I close my eyes, I can almost still smell the sweetness wafting through the air.

PREP TIME · 25 minutes

COOK TIME · 1 hour

- 1 package (4 oz.) German Sweet Chocolate
- ½ cup boiling water
- 1 cup butter
- 2 cups sugar
- 4 egg yolks
- 2½ cups sifted cake flour (or 2¼ cups all-purpose flour mixed with ¼ cup corn starch)
- 1 teaspoon baking soda
- ½ teaspoon salt
- 1 teaspoon vanilla extract
- 1 cup full-fat buttermilk (not reduced fat)
- 4 egg whites, stiffly beaten

Coconut Pecan Frosting

- 1 cup evaporated milk
- 1 cup sugar
- 3 egg yolks
- ½ cup real butter
- 1 teaspoon vanilla extract
- 1 ⅓ cups flaked, sweetened coconut
- 1 cup chopped pecans

INSTRUCTIONS

1 Preheat the oven to 350 degrees.

2 Prepare three 8- or 9-inch round cake pans by greasing well and lining with parchment paper on the bottom.

3 In a small bowl, pour the boiling water over the German sweet chocolate.

4 Stir and let cool slightly.

5 In a large bowl, cream the butter and sugar until light and fluffy.

6 Add the egg yolks, beating well.

7 In a medium bowl, stir together the flour, soda, and salt.

8 Blend the vanilla into the melted chocolate.

9 Alternate adding the dry ingredients, buttermilk, and chocolate mixture to the butter and sugar mixture, beating well until smooth.

10 Gently fold in the stiffly beaten egg whites and pour into your prepared cake pans.

11 Bake for 30 to 40 minutes, being careful not to over bake.

12 To make the frosting, combine the evaporated milk, sugar, egg yolks, butter, and vanilla in a medium size saucepan.

13 Cook over medium, low heat, stirring constantly until the mixture begins to thicken.

14 This will take about 10 to 12 minutes.

15 Remove from heat and add coconut and pecans.

16 Beat well until it cools and is a consistency that will allow for spreading.

17 Cool cakes and frost in between the layers and the top with coconut pecan frosting.

18 Leave the frosting off the sides.

19 Store in a cake dome until ready to serve.

YIELDS · 12-15 slices

UTTERLY DEADLY KEY LIME PIE

Karen

I made this as a brand-new bride just after we'd visited Florida for our first real vacation the year we were married. I saw this dessert everywhere in Florida. Once home, every key lime recipe I read stressed the importance of using real key limes, not just any old lime from the grocery store and they were right! If you can't find fresh key limes, you can usually find bottled key lime juice. This dessert is a heavenly marriage of a sweet, buttery graham cracker crust and a creamy, bright citrus-y middle. You may use canned whipped cream for topping if desired instead of the fresh whipped cream.

PREP TIME · 25 minutes
COOK TIME · 25 minutes plus 4 hours to chill

Crust

- 1¼ cup graham cracker crumbs
- 2½ tablespoons sugar
- 5 tablespoons butter, melted

Filling

- 1 can (14 oz.) sweetened condensed milk
- 4 large egg yolks
- 1 tablespoon lime zest
- ½ cup key lime juice (freshly squeezed or bottled)

Topping

- 1 cup heavy whipping cream, chilled
- 2 tablespoons powdered sugar
- 8 thin lime slices, for garnish

Therefore, as we have opportunity, let us do good to all people,

especially to those who belong to the family of believers.

GALATIANS 6:10

1   Preheat the oven to 350 degrees.

2   In a medium bowl, mix the graham cracker crumbs, sugar, and melted butter.

3   Using the back of a large spoon, press crumb mixture into the bottom and sides of a 9-inch pie dish.

4   Bake for 10 minutes.

5   Remove from the oven and let cool on a rack. Leave the oven on.

6   In another medium bowl, using a hand mixer on medium speed, mix the condensed milk and egg yolks until slightly thickened.

7   Blend in the lime zest and key lime juice until smooth.

8   Pour the filling into the crust and bake for 18 to 23 minutes, until edges are set and the center is just slightly jiggly.

9   Transfer pie to a cooling rack and let cool completely before refrigerating at least 4 hours or overnight.

10   When ready to serve, using a chilled metal bowl and chilled beaters, beat the whipping cream and sugar with a hand mixer on medium-high speed until soft peaks form.

11   Serve pie slices topped with the whipped cream and garnished with lime slices. So pretty!

YIELDS · 8 servings

HOT FUDGE SUNDAE CAKE

Karen

This is a super easy dessert to make when you have company. A layer of delicious, ooey-gooey warm fudge settles to the bottom as it bakes. To serve, cut into squares and flip them upside down onto dessert plates. Top with vanilla bean ice cream.

PREP TIME · 15 minutes
COOK TIME · 35-40 minutes

- 1 cup flour
- ¾ cup sugar
- ¼ cup plus 2 tablespoons cocoa powder, divided
- 2 teaspoons baking powder
- ¼ teaspoon salt
- ½ cup whole milk
- 3 tablespoons olive oil
- 1 teaspoon vanilla extract (can use almond, orange, or mint too–Yum!)
- 1 cup chopped walnuts or pecans (optional)
- 1 cup brown sugar, firmly packed
- 1¾ cup boiling water
- Vanilla or other favorite ice cream for topping

INSTRUCTIONS

1 Preheat the oven to 350 degrees.

2 In an 8- or 9-inch ungreased square pan, combine the flour, sugar, 2 tablespoons cocoa powder, baking powder, and salt.

3 Add milk, oil, and vanilla, blending until smooth.

4 Stir in walnuts.

5 In a small bowl, combine brown sugar and ¼ cup cocoa and sprinkle over the top.

6 Pour boiling water over the entire pan and do NOT stir.

7 Bake at 350 degrees for 35 to 40 minutes until lightly set.

8 Cut into squares and flip them upside down onto dessert plates.

9 Serve warm topped with ice cream.

YIELDS · 6-8 servings

SIMPLY SOURDOUGH

"If you really want to make a friend, go round someone's house with a freshly baked loaf of sourdough bread!"

— CHRIS GEIGER

The recent pandemic prompted many people who were stuck at home to try their hand at some old-fashioned skills such as knitting, gardening, and making sourdough baked goods. Not only are these baked goods rather tasty, they have the added bonus of being better for us, especially being gentler on our digestive systems. Our ancestors knew what they were doing! Happy sourdough baking to you!

Sourdough Basics

Every sourdough recipe must have a sourdough starter, which is why the very first recipe in this section is a sourdough starter.

You'll notice that we switch to weighing ingredients for this recipe. This helps to make sure that the measurements are precise and increases the chance of a successful and active sourdough starter. (You can purchase a kitchen scale online or in the kitchen tool aisle of most supermarkets to help you weigh the ingredients accurately.)

IMPORTANT NOTE: In each of the recipes in this section, the list of ingredients includes either the term "active sourdough starter" or "sourdough discard." *Active sourdough starter* indicates that the starter has been fed before using it in the recipe. *Sourdough discard* means a portion of the starter that you'd otherwise discard before feeding. It is important to note that you *can* use active sourdough starter in a recipe that calls for sourdough discard; but you *cannot* use sourdough discard in a recipe that calls for active sourdough starter.

SOURDOUGH STARTER RECIPE

Macey

This is my tried-and-true sourdough starter recipe that yields an active starter every time. Whether you're a novice bread-maker or a veteran, this recipe is easy to follow and yields great results. Shoutout to the famous Jessa Greenfield for the original recipe, which I tweaked to best fit my sourdough needs!

PREP TIME · 5 days

- 512 grams of flour, divided
- 472 grams of water, divided
- Large ceramic container
- Cheese cloth (to cover container)
- Rubber band (to secure cheese cloth if necessary)
- Wooden or silicone utensil (to incorporate flour and water)
- Kitchen scale

INSTRUCTIONS

Day One

1 Pour 128 grams of flour and 118 grams of water into a large container and stir until smooth.

2 Cover with cheesecloth and secure with a rubber band. You can also cover loosely with plastic wrap.

3 Place in a room that keeps a steady temperature of 70 to 75 degrees.

4 Let sit for 24 hours.

Day Two

1 You may notice some small bubbles appear. This is a good sign that the yeast is feeding on the sugar present in the flour and releasing carbon dioxide and alcohol.

2 If you notice a vinegar smell, that is okay! Add 128 grams of flour and 118 grams of water to your starter.

3 Mix until smooth and free of lumps.

4 Cover with cheesecloth or plastic wrap, and let it sit for 24 hours at a constant temperature of 70 to 75 degrees.

Day Three

1   The whole surface of the starter should have bubbles. It should also look like it has grown in volume. The starter should smell strongly of vinegar.

2   Add 128 grams of flour and 118 grams of water to your starter.

3   Mix until smooth and free of lumps.

4   Cover with cheesecloth or plastic wrap, and let it sit for 24 hours at a constant temperature of 70 to 75 degrees.

Day Four

1   You should notice even larger bubbles. The starter should be thinner in consistency than in days one through three. The smell should be very sour.

2   Add 128 grams of flour and 118 grams of water to your starter.

3   Mix until smooth and free of lumps.

4   Cover with cheesecloth or plastic wrap, and let it sit for 24 hours at a constant temperature of 70 to 75 degrees.

Day Five

1   Your starter should have doubled in size and be very bubbly and frothy. When you stir your starter, it should feel and look web-like.

2   Congratulations! You've successfully made your sourdough starter!

3   Going forward, you should refresh your starter at least 2 to 3 times a week.

To refresh your starter

1   Discard about half (usually by making a recipe, sharing with a friend, or throwing away or in your compost pile—our pigs love sourdough discard!) and add equal amounts of flour and water in grams to the mixture, incorporating both ingredients until smooth and free of lumps.

2   Being consistent with discarding and feeding is important to maintain the health of your starter! If you want to stop the fermentation process (*i.e.* you cannot discard and refresh it as frequently as needed), then you can place your container in the fridge.

3   Before placing the starter in the fridge, refresh your starter by adding equal amounts of flour and water in grams, incorporating both ingredients until smooth and free of lumps. I usually add about 30 to 50 grams of each.

4   I have left my starter in my fridge for up to 30 days without harming it.

YIELDS · 1 sourdough starter

SOURDOUGH PIE CRUST

Macey

One of the favorite cooking combinations that Grandma Kit—that's Karen, if you didn't know—and I have done is her homemade chicken pot pie filling with my pie crust recipe. This past August when she and Pops—my father-in-law, Todd—came to visit us on the farm, my husband asked if she would make her famous chicken pot pie and if I would make a homemade pie crust for it! It was the best collaboration of 2023 in my book! This pie crust recipe can be used for sweet or savory, and it's also a sourdough recipe that can be used the same day!

PREP TIME · 15 minutes, plus 1 hour to chill

COOK TIME · 45 minutes

- 1½ cups flour
- 1 teaspoon salt
- 1½ tablespoons sugar
- 1 cup butter, cold and cubed
- 1 cup active sourdough starter

INSTRUCTIONS

1. Cube your butter and leave it in your fridge until you're ready to use it.

2. In a mixing bowl, mix together the flour, salt, and sugar until combined.

3. Use your hands to work the cold butter into the flour mixture until it is in pea sized pieces.

4. Add the active sourdough starter and mix to combine until the dough begins to come together.

5. Turn out the dough onto a floured surface and knead until the flour is all incorporated, but do not overwork it.

6. Some chunks of butter will still be present, and that is okay! Divide the dough in half and wrap in plastic.

7. Chill dough in the fridge for at least 1 hour, and up to 3 days. You can also freeze for later use.

8. When ready to use, place chilled dough on a floured surface. Roll into a circle to fit your pie dish.

9. Place the dough into a greased and floured pie dish. Do not stretch the dough to make it fit because the dough will shrink back down. Let the edges hang over the side of the dish and trim around the edges with scissors to remove excess.

10. Fill with your desired filling and proceed with your recipe!

YIELDS · Two 9-inch pie crusts

FOUR-HERB SOUP CRACKERS

Macey

It's a cold, rainy day today as I'm writing this recipe, and there is nothing that I love more on a cold, rainy day than warm soup. And what does warm soup need? Soup crackers of course! This is my take on a recipe that I found on a social media site. With this combination of herbs, the flavor is unmatched, and these crackers work for tomato-based soups as well as milk and cheese based soups. Such a versatile soup cracker! Sometimes, we just eat the crackers themselves without soup included because they're so flavorful!

PREP TIME · 10 minutes

COOK TIME · 30-60 minutes

- ¾ cup sourdough discard
- 2 tablespoons butter, melted
- ¾ teaspoon salt, divided
- ½ teaspoon basil
- ½ teaspoon rosemary
- ½ teaspoon oregano
- ½ teaspoon parsley

INSTRUCTIONS

1   Preheat your oven to 325 degrees, and line a small sheet pan with parchment paper.

2   In a bowl, add sourdough discard, melted butter, ½ teaspoon of salt, and the dried herbs and stir until combined.

3   Use a spatula to spread the mixture in a thin, even layer on the parchment paper.

4   Bake for 10 minutes.

5   Remove from the oven and score the crackers.

6   Bake for an additional 20 minutes or until the crackers are golden brown, checking often to make sure they don't burn.

7   Let cool completely before breaking into squares.

YIELDS · 4 servings

MELT-IN-YOUR-MOUTH BISCUITS

Macey

My biscuit recipe is one of my favorite sourdough recipes to make for a couple of reasons. First, I can discard some of my sourdough starter, and I make a yummy biscuit in the process. Second, usually sourdough recipes take several hours to make, if not days, and this recipe is one that you can decide to make on a whim without much planning and preparation. I usually make bacon, egg, and cheese biscuits on Saturday mornings for my boys using this from-scratch biscuit recipe. Five star reviews every time!

PREP TIME · 30 minutes
COOK TIME · 10-15 minutes

- 2 cups all-purpose flour
- 2 teaspoons baking powder
- 1¼ teaspoon salt
- ½ teaspoon baking soda
- 1 cup butter, cold and cubed into ¼-inch pieces
- 1 cup sourdough discard
- ½ cup milk
- 3 tablespoons bacon grease, melted

INSTRUCTIONS

1   Preheat your oven to 400 degrees.

2   Line a large baking sheet with parchment paper. Set aside.

3   In a mixing bowl, combine flour, baking powder, salt, and baking soda.

4   Using your hands, incorporate the butter into the flour mixture until you have pea-sized pieces.

5   Add the sourdough discard and the milk to the flour mixture.

6   Using an electric stand mixer with a dough hook, mix on low until a dough forms (about 3 to 5 minutes).

7   Turn out your dough onto a floured counter.

8   Knead the dough for about 1 minute, and then form the dough into a 1-inch-thick circle.

9   Use a biscuit cutter (or a cup if you do not have a biscuit cutter) to cut out the biscuits.

10 Transfer the cutouts to the large lined baking sheet.

11 Using a silicone baking brush, brush the bacon grease onto each biscuit.

12 Bake for 10 to 15 minutes, until the tops are lightly brown.

13 Serve warm and with your favorite toppings!

YIELDS · 8-10 servings

HAMBURGER BUNS

Macey

When my husband and I decided to eat healthier after we got married, we began to eat burgers without buns because of the harmful additives and potential pesticides in commercial gluten. Did you know that some people are not gluten intolerant but sensitive to pesticides and other harmful additives found in commercial gluten products? How crazy! With all this said, I love a good burger, which includes the bun! It's part of the experience! So, I went on the hunt for a good, sourdough hamburger bun recipe, and boy did I find one! This recipe is also versatile, and you can make it into a hotdog bun as well!

PREP TIME · 2 ½ hours

COOK TIME · 15-20 minutes

- 2¾ cups flour
- ⅛ cup sugar
- ¾ tablespoon instant yeast
- 1 teaspoon salt
- ½ cup sourdough discard
- 1 egg
- ⅛ cup of olive oil
- ¾ cup cold water
- 4 tablespoons butter, melted
- 4 tablespoons sesame seeds
- Kitchen scale

INSTRUCTIONS

1   In a stand mixer using the dough hook attachment, combine flour, sugar, yeast, and salt.

2   Add sourdough discard, egg, oil, and cold water to the flour mixture.

3   Mix on low until combined.

4   Increase speed to medium and knead for 8 to 10 minutes.

5   Place the dough in a proofing basket, cover with a damp tea towel, and allow it to rise for 1 hour, until it doubles in size.

6   Preheat your oven to 400 degrees.

7   Line a large baking sheet with parchment paper.

8   Using a kitchen scale, divide the dough into 3-ounce portions and roll into balls. Place each dough ball, seam side down, onto the parchment lined baking sheet.

9   Cover and allow to rise another hour.

10   Bake uncovered for 15 to 20 minutes or until done.

11   Remove from oven and brush the tops with butter and sprinkle 1 teaspoon of sesame seeds on each bun.

12   Allow to cool before cutting.

YIELDS · About 12 buns

IRISH SODA BREAD

Macey

Saint Patrick's Day has always been one of my favorite "small" holidays, if not my very favorite. I grew up in a tiny town in rural South Georgia, and I attended school in a neighboring city—Dublin. So many of my favorite memories were made in Dublin with my best friends Megan and Alicia. At the top of that list of favorite memories are the ones where I spent time with loved ones during the Saint Patrick's Day festivities. From the Leprechaun Road Race to green lemonade at the local Chick-Fil-A to the used book sale at the library to the Saint Patrick's Day parade—my hometown of Dublin goes all out, all March long. There are festivities scheduled each day of March, reminding me of a Hallmark movie or perhaps an Irish version of Stars Hollow. Enjoy this Irish soda bread—one of my favorite authentic Irish recipes to make and inspired by my hometown!

PREP TIME · 15 minutes

COOK TIME · 40 minutes

- 1 cup sourdough discard
- 1 egg
- 2 tablespoons butter, melted
- ½ cup buttermilk, plus extra for brushing the top of the bread
- 2½ cups flour
- ½ cup rolled oats
- ½ teaspoon baking soda
- 2 teaspoons baking powder
- 1 tablespoon sugar
- 1 teaspoon salt

Hospitality Hack

One of the most creative ideas I've ever heard was to have a regular night of hosting at your home for Saturday night supper and board games and a movie for the kiddos. Everyone brings their leftovers from the week and puts on a smorgasbord. Someone else's leftovers don't seem like leftovers to you. They seem like something new! Round out the meal by offering a tossed salad and a simple dessert.

1 Place your Dutch oven and lid inside your oven and preheat the oven to 400 degrees.

2 Whisk together your sourdough discard, egg, butter, and buttermilk.

3 If you do not have buttermilk on hand, you can make buttermilk by mixing ½ cup milk with 1½ teaspoons apple cider vinegar, white vinegar, or lemon juice and allowing it to sit on your countertop for about 10 minutes or until it curdles.

4 Make sure to make a little extra to brush on your bread right before baking.

5 In a separate bowl, whisk together your flour, oats, baking soda, baking powder, sugar, and salt.

6 Combine the wet and dry ingredients in a stand mixer using a dough hook.

7 Mix on low for a couple of minutes until the dough forms into a ball.

8 If your dough is too dry, add more buttermilk.

9 If your dough is too sticky, add some more flour.

10 Cut two strips of parchment paper the width of your Dutch oven and long enough to come up over the sides.

11 Arrange the parchment paper in a cross shape on your countertop.

12 Place the ball of dough in the center of the parchment paper cross and score the top of the dough with an "X" making sure that you cut at least ½ way through the dough.

13 Brush the top of the dough with the reserved buttermilk.

14 Using caution, remove the preheated Dutch oven.

15 Grasping the sides of the parchment paper, use it like a sling to pick up the dough.

16 Place the parchment paper with the dough inside it in the hot Dutch oven.

17 Bake at 400 degrees for 35 to 40 minutes or until the top is golden brown.

18 Let cool for 15 minutes before cutting.

19 Enjoy with your favorite toppings!

YIELDS · 1 loaf

SANDWICH BREAD

My Saturday routine is to make a loaf of sandwich bread because it is so versatile, and you can add in anything to suit your taste. Our favorite things to add in are mozzarella cheese and jalapenos. These are included in the recipe below, but you can add in whatever you prefer, or leave it plain. There are also many different toppings that are simply delicious like butter, a fruit spread, cream cheese, and more. It's also an amazing bread to use for avocado toast, any kind of sandwich, and when bread crumbles are needed in a recipe. Of all the sourdough items that I make, this is one that my family cannot seem to live without!

PREP TIME · 12-18 hours

COOK TIME · 55 minutes

- 1 cup active sourdough starter
- 1 cup lukewarm water
- 2 teaspoons salt
- 3 cups + 2 tablespoons all-purpose flour (or any flour that you would like)
- 3 tablespoons butter, melted

Add-ins (optional)

- ½ cup mozzarella cheese
- ¼ cup pickled jalapenos, chopped

SOUL SOOTHER

Even though all of our sourdough recipes can be completed in a stand mixer, we highly recommend kneading your dough by hand. Kneading is a self-soothing technique and can reduce feelings of anxiety and depression.

INSTRUCTIONS

1   Combine the sourdough starter, water, and salt in a mixing bowl.

2   Stir and let stand for 5 minutes.

3   Next, add in any additional flavors you'd like. We prefer ½ cup of mozzarella and ¼ cup chopped pickled jalapenos.

4   Add the flour, mixing to form the dough.

5   When all the flour is added, cover your dough loosely with a towel and let your dough sit for 8 to 12 hours (or overnight) at room temperature to rise.

6   After the first rise, sprinkle 2 tablespoons of flour onto a countertop and knead it into your dough, about 5 minutes or until all the flour is incorporated.

7   Allow your dough to rise a second time, about 3 to 5 hours.

8   Preheat your oven to 450 degrees with your Dutch oven and lid inside to preheat as well.

9   Once your oven comes to temperature, take out your Dutch oven, line with parchment paper, and place bread in your Dutch oven.

10   Score your bread and place the lid back on the Dutch oven.

11   Return to your oven and cook at 450 degrees with the lid on for 40 minutes.

12   Then, remove the lid from the Dutch oven and turn your oven down to 350 degrees.

13   Cook for another 10 minutes.

14   Remove from oven and brush with melted butter.

15   Let cool on a bread rack.

16   Cut once cooled, and enjoy!

YIELDS · 1 medium loaf

SOURDOUGH PRETZELS

Macey

I love to pair these sourdough pretzels with my Spinach Three Cheese Dip *(see the recipe on page 28). These pretzels are the perfect dipping tool to transport my decadent cheese dip to another world. My recommendation is to always make these two recipes together. Your taste buds and your loved ones will thank you! However, feel free to make these pretzels and dip them into your dipping dish of choice.*

PREP TIME · 1 hour
COOK TIME · 20 minutes

- ¾ cup milk
- 1½ cups sourdough discard
- 4 tablespoons softened butter, divided
- 3 cups all-purpose flour
- 1 tablespoon granulated sugar
- 1½ teaspoons salt
- 2 teaspoons instant yeast
- 1 tablespoon baking soda
- 2 tablespoons water
- Coarse sea salt, to taste
- 2 tablespoons sesame seeds

And let us consider how we may spur one another on toward love and good deeds…

HEBREWS 10:24

1 In a stand mixer, add milk, sourdough discard, 2 tablespoons softened butter, flour, granulated sugar, salt, and instant yeast.

2 Knead until a dough forms and is smooth, about 10 minutes.

3 You may need to add small amounts of water to make a cohesive dough.

4 Put the dough in a proofing basket, cover with a damp tea towel, and allow it to rest for 45 minutes.

5 Preheat your oven to 350 degrees.

6 Line a large baking sheet with parchment paper.

7 Roll the dough out until it's about ½ inch thick.

8 Cut the dough into 12 equal pieces.

9 Roll each piece of dough into a "rope" about 18 inches long.

10 Form each dough rope into a pretzel.

11 Lay each pretzel on your lined baking sheet.

12 In a small dish, combine water and baking soda and brush on each pretzel.

13 Sprinkle salt on each of the wet pretzels.

14 Bake at 350 degrees for 20 minutes or until golden brown.

15 Remove to a cooling rack.

16 Brush the warm pretzels with 2 tablespoons of melted butter and sprinkle sesame seeds on each wet pretzel.

17 Serve and enjoy!

YIELDS · 6-8 pretzels

STUFFED CRUST PIZZA

Macey

When my son was born, my husband and I became intentional about creating traditions in our home. One of our traditions is weekly homemade stuffed crust pizza night! Every Friday night, we take the dough that I prepared that morning, load it with cheese sticks in the crust and with our favorite toppings, and within minutes, we have a delicious weekend meal! Growing up, my family had weekly pizza nights, but we went to our local pizza joint in McRae, GA called Village Pizza. So, it's been fun to recreate those core memories with our family at our home instead. An extra shoutout to Mitchell's dad, Todd, for the string cheese idea! This is one recipe I highly suggest working into your weekly routine!

PREP TIME · 8-12 hours
COOK TIME · 15 minutes

- ¾ cup sourdough discard
- 1¼ cup water
- 1 teaspoon salt
- 3½ cups plus 2 tablespoons all-purpose flour
- 10 to 12 string cheese sticks
- 14 ounces pizza sauce
- 1½ cups shredded mozzarella cheese (or shredded three cheese Mexican cheese)
- 1 pound bacon, cooked and chopped
- 1 pound ground spicy pork sausage, cooked and crumbled
- 15 pepperonis
- ½ medium Vidalia onion, chopped
- 4 tablespoons butter
- 1 teaspoon garlic salt
- 4 teaspoons parmesan cheese
- Avocado oil cooking spray

1   In a stand mixer with a dough hook attachment, add sourdough discard, water, and salt and mix well until combined.

2   Add the flour and knead until a dough forms.

3   Put your dough in a proofing basket, and cover with a damp tea towel.

4   Allow to rise in a warm environment for 8 to 12 hours.

5   After your dough has risen, knead 2 tablespoons of flour into the dough and allow it to sit while you prepare the toppings.

6   Preheat your oven to 500 degrees (yes, you read that correctly!).

7   Spray the bottom and sides of a large baking sheet with avocado oil cooking spray.

8   Lay your dough in the middle of the baking sheet and begin to gently stretch the dough (you can use a rolling pin) until it covers the entirety of the sheet pan and overlaps on the sides.

9   Line the edge of the dough with the string cheese sticks.

10   Once your entire dough has been "framed" by the string cheese, fold the edges of the dough over the string cheese and press down firmly making sure that the string cheese is covered by dough.

11   Next, pour about 14 ounces of pizza sauce onto the dough and spread until the dough is covered up to the crust.

12   You can use more or less depending on your preference.

13   Then, cover the sauce with cheese.

14   Again, you can use more or less depending on your preference.

15   Next, add all your toppings: crumbled bacon, ground sausage, pepperonis, and chopped onion.

16   Once you have put all desired toppings on your pizza (feel free to add different ones based on your tastes!), place the sheet pan in the oven and cook for 10 to 15 minutes or until your pizza is cooked thoroughly and your cheese is bubbly and browned.

17   While the pizza is cooking, combine the melted butter and garlic salt.

18   Brush the garlic butter mixture onto the crust of the pizza once you take it out of the oven.

19   While the crust is still wet with butter, sprinkle parmesan cheese on the crust.

20   Cut into slices with a pizza cutter and enjoy!

YIELDS · One large (26 x 18-inch) pizza

JUST-LIKE-THE-FAIR CORN DOGS

Macey

Mitchell and I have made a commitment to eat healthier and to pay attention to what we put into our bodies. Once upon a time, we both ate whatever! However, we slowly began to cut items out of our diets based on inflammatory seed oils and other nasty chemicals and harmful additives, but let me tell you, I missed a good ole corn dog from the fair. I had my fair share of fair corn dogs in the last five years too, mind you, because they are just that good, and I wasn't ready to give them up. So, when I was introduced to sourdough, I began to wonder if I could make a healthy, yet just as tasty, corn dog version. Look no further with this recipe! Healthy for your gut and as healthy as a corn dog can be—that's all a carb-loving girl can hope for!

PREP TIME · 15 minutes

COOK TIME · 30 minutes

- 2 to 3 cups avocado oil or extra virgin olive oil
- 1 cup cornmeal
- 1 cup all-purpose flour, plus 2 tablespoons for coating
- ½ teaspoon salt
- ½ teaspoon Cajun seasoning
- ¼ teaspoon pepper
- ⅛ teaspoon ground cloves
- 2 teaspoons baking powder
- 1 cup active sourdough starter
- 1 large egg
- 1 cup milk
- 8 brats, fully cooked
- 8 wooden skewers
- 1 empty 32-ounce jar

INSTRUCTIONS

1   Heat your avocado oil in a large cast iron skillet over medium heat.

2   While your oil is warming up, whisk together your dry ingredients in a 32-ounce jar: corn-meal, flour, salt, Cajun seasoning, pepper, cloves, and baking powder.

3   Add wet ingredients to your dry ingredient mixture: sourdough starter, egg, and milk.

4   Stir until combined.

5   Put a wooden skewer lengthwise through your brats leaving enough of the skewer to hold on to.

6   Put 2 tablespoons of flour in a shallow dish and coat your brats in the flour (this helps your batter adhere to your brats).

7   Dip each brat into the batter, dipping straight down until the brat is fully coated then twirling and swirling as you pull it up and out of the jar.

8   Place each brat in the oil.

9   I am "shallow" frying in this recipe, which means you need to use tongs to turn the corn dog over on its other side once one side finishes cooking.

10 Cook until dark golden, about 2 to 5 minutes on each side.

11 Enjoy with *Uncle Bo's Honey Mustard* on page 220 or your favorite dressing!

YIELDS · 8 servings

MOLASSES COOKIES

Macey

We have a Mennonite farmer's market near us where we buy a lot of our groceries, and they always have home-made sorghum cookies. I tried to recreate this cookie recipe with molasses, and these are now my husband and son's favorite cookies that I make! I'm even turning them into Scooby snacks for my son's second birthday party! We will most likely sneak a few (or a lot) before the party starts because they're just that good!

PREP TIME · 2-24 hours
COOK TIME · 10 minutes

- 2 cups all-purpose flour
- 2 teaspoons baking soda
- ½ teaspoon salt
- 2 teaspoons ground ginger powder
- 2 teaspoons cinnamon
- ½ teaspoon pumpkin pie spice
- ⅛ teaspoon nutmeg
- 12 tablespoons butter, softened but not melted
- ½ cup granulated sugar, plus ½ cup for rolling the cookie dough balls
- ½ cup brown sugar
- 1 egg
- ⅓ cup unsulphured molasses
- 2 teaspoons vanilla extract
- ½ cup sourdough starter, active or discard

INSTRUCTIONS

1   Combine all dry ingredients in a bowl: the flour, baking soda, salt, and spices. Mix well.

2   In a separate bowl, mix together the softened butter and both sugars.

3   You can cut into 1 tablespoon cubes before adding it to the sugar to mix everything more smoothly.

4   In your butter and sugar mixture, beat in the egg followed by the molasses and vanilla.

5   Add the sourdough starter to your butter and sugar mixture. Mix thoroughly.

6   Gradually add the dry ingredients to the wet mixture, stirring until combined. Be careful not to overmix.

7   Cover and refrigerate the dough to chill for at least 2 hours up to a couple of days.

8   Use plastic wrap to prevent the dough from drying out.

9   The longer that the sourdough is able to sit and ferment the healthier the cookies are for you—well, as healthy as cookies can be! You can freeze the raw cookie dough for up to 3 months.

10   Keep the cookie dough in your fridge until you're ready to form and bake the cookies.

11   Preheat your oven to 350 degrees.

12   Line a large baking sheet with parchment paper.

13   Add about ½ cup of white sugar to a small bowl.

14   Using your hands, roll the dough into 1-inch balls.

15   Toss the balls in the sugar until they're lightly but evenly coated.

16   Place your cookie dough balls on your baking sheet, and space them about three inches apart.

17   Bake for 9 to 10 minutes or until the cookie is done.

18   Remove from the oven and allow to rest for at least 5 minutes.

19   Enjoy with a glass of cold milk!

YIELDS · 30-32 cookies

CHOCOLATE CHIP COOKIES

Macey

These chocolate chip cookies are to die for! The sourdough twang makes them simply the perfect combination of sweet and tangy, and the fermentation process helps them to be healthier for our guts and more easily processed by our bodies! Enjoy this sweet treat without making your body feel yucky!

PREP TIME · 10 minutes
COOK TIME · 10 minutes

- 1 cup butter
- ½ cup granulated sugar
- ½ cup brown sugar
- 1 egg
- 2 teaspoons vanilla extract
- ¾ cup active sourdough starter
- 2 cups all-purpose flour
- 1 teaspoon salt
- ½ teaspoon baking soda
- ¼ teaspoon baking powder
- 3 cups chocolate chunks

INSTRUCTIONS

1 Preheat your oven to 350 degrees and line a large baking sheet with parchment paper.

2 In a mixer with a paddle attachment, mix butter and both types of sugars together until light and fluffy.

3 Add egg and mix until well incorporated.

4 Add vanilla and sourdough starter and mix until just combined.

5 In a separate bowl, mix dry ingredients together.

6 Add the dry ingredients to the wet ingredients and mix until combined.

7 Add chocolate chunks and mix on low so that they are gently incorporated.

8 Roll the dough into 1-inch balls.

9 Place cookies on a baking sheet about 2 inches apart, and bake for 10 minutes or until the edges begin to harden/turn golden.

10 Enjoy warm with a glass of milk!

YIELDS · About 24 cookies

MULTI-BERRY AND PEACH COBBLER

Macey

Every year in October, my family and I would go to the Georgia National Fair in Perry, GA. It was such a big deal in our neck of the woods that my parents would excuse me from school to attend. I loved walking around with my family, riding fair rides, eating delicious food, and checking out all of the vendors, especially the Georgia Grown building. My cousins, Dylan and Derek, were members of the FFA program, and oftentimes, I would hang out in the barns with them and their friends (and their cows!) before and after their cow shows. One of our favorite things to do between cow shows, especially my dad's, was to find a booth that sold peach cobbler. Nothing says "Georgia" like peach cobbler, and this is my family's twist on this tried-and-true Southern recipe! Make sure to use Georgia peaches; they're the best!

PREP TIME · 15 minutes
COOK TIME · 45 minutes

- ½ cup butter
- 1 cup sugar
- ½ teaspoon salt
- 1 cup flour
- 2 teaspoons baking powder
- ½ cup milk
- ¼ cup sourdough discard
- 1 can (15 oz.) of peaches with juice
- 2 cups of your favorite berries

INSTRUCTIONS

1. Preheat your oven to 350 degrees.

2. Place the butter in a 9 x 13-inch baking dish and put your baking dish in the oven to melt the butter. You can do this while your oven preheats.

3. In a stand mixer, mix your sugar, salt, flour, baking powder, milk, and sourdough discard until well combined.

4. Take your baking dish out of the oven and pour your batter into the dish, stirring a little.

5. Dump the whole can of peaches and your berries onto the batter with juices included. We like to use blueberries, strawberries, and blackberries or raspberries.

6. Do not stir or mix.

7. Bake for about 45 minutes or until done.

8. Enjoy topped with your favorite ice cream!

YIELDS · One 9 x 13-inch cobbler

LEMON BLUEBERRY SCONES

Macey

Every time that I make these scones, I think of my brother-in-law and sister-in-law, Spencer and Mariange. They love lemons, and their kitchen is decorated in pale yellow, featuring lemon adornments. I love lemons myself and all things yellow. Just making these scones and zesting the lemons for it uplifts my mood. These are light and delicious and the perfect addition to high tea!

PREP TIME · 5 minutes
COOK TIME · 15-20 minutes

- 1 cup almond flour
- 1 cup all-purpose flour
- ½ cup granulated sugar
- 2 teaspoons baking powder
- ½ teaspoon salt
- ½ cup butter, cold and cut in cubes
- ⅓ cup sourdough discard
- 2 eggs
- 2 lemons, zested
- 1 teaspoon vanilla extract
- 2 cups frozen blueberries

INSTRUCTIONS

1   Preheat the oven to 350 degrees.

2   Line a large baking sheet with parchment paper.

3   Whisk all the dry ingredients in a large bowl.

4   Add the cold cubed butter to the dry ingredient mixture, breaking up the cubes into pea-sized pieces with your hands.

5   Mix the sourdough discard, eggs, lemon zest, and vanilla in another small bowl.

6   Add the wet mixture to the dry ingredients along with the frozen blueberries, stirring until combined.

7   On a lightly floured surface, form your batter into a long log 2 inches in diameter.

8   Cut into 10 triangles using a pastry cutter.

9   Bake for 15 to 20 minutes or until they are cooked thoroughly and slightly brown.

YIELDS · 10 scones

BANANA BREAD

Macey

Banana bread is such a grounding dessert and warms you from the inside out. I love making it on a cold winter night and enjoying it with a cup of coffee or tea by a crackling fire. It's also a great dessert to make when all of those bananas you just bought all ripen at the same time!

PREP TIME · 15 minutes

COOK TIME · 1 hour

- 2 cups all-purpose flour
- ½ teaspoon baking soda
- ½ teaspoon salt
- ½ cup butter, room temperature
- 1 cup brown sugar

- 2 large eggs, room temperature
- 1 teaspoon vanilla
- 4 ripe bananas, mashed
- 1 cup sourdough discard
- Avocado oil cooking spray

INSTRUCTIONS

1   Preheat your oven to 350 degrees.

2   Spray the bottom and sides of a 9 x 5-inch bread loaf pan.

3   In a medium bowl, combine flour, baking soda, and salt and set aside.

4   In a stand mixer, add the butter and sugar.

5   Mix on medium speed until fully incorporated, about 2 minutes.

6   Add the eggs, vanilla, and bananas.

7   Mix until only a few lumps remain.

8   You may need to scrape the bowl while mixing to ensure that everything is incorporated.

9   Add in the flour mixture and the sourdough starter and gently mix to combine.

10 Bake at 350 degrees for 55 to 60 minutes or until a toothpick inserted into the middle has only a few crumbs that cling to it. Do not overbake.

11 I put a sheet pan underneath in case some of the dough spills over out of the bread loaf pan.

12 Allow to cool for at least 10 minutes before cutting.

YIELDS · One 9 x 5 loaf

CINNAMON ROLLS

Macey

These cinnamon rolls are a staple in our house, and this is a recipe that is often requested by my family and friends (rivaled only by my famous carrot cake). Although the recipe takes time, these are simple to make. Our family tradition is to make these cinnamon rolls on Christmas Eve night and bake them on Christmas Day as a family. I love recipes that bring all of my loved ones into the kitchen and around the table! Add optional pumpkin puree for a delightful fall addition to this sweet treat!

PREP TIME · 45 minutes, plus 10 hours to overnight to rise

COOK TIME · 30 minutes

Rolls

- 1½ cups active sourdough starter
- 2 eggs
- 1 cup lukewarm water
- ⅓ cup brown sugar
- ¼ cup avocado oil
- 1 teaspoon salt
- 5 cups all-purpose flour

Filling

- 4 tablespoons butter, melted
- 2 tablespoons cinnamon
- ¾ cup brown sugar
- 6 ounces pumpkin puree, optional

Icing

- 6 ounces cream cheese, softened
- ½ cup butter, softened
- 3 cups powdered sugar, sifted
- 2 teaspoons vanilla extract
- ½ teaspoon salt

SOUL SOOTHER

Traditions are important in fostering the four "b's," which are: our senses of being, belonging, believing, and benevolence. Traditions also provide a source of structure and comfort. Whether they incorporate food or not, make sure to come up with your own traditions for you and your loved ones!

INSTRUCTIONS

1   To make the rolls, combine the first six ingredients into a bowl and mix well.

2   Then, add the flour and mix.

3   Turn dough out onto a lightly floured surface and knead for 10 minutes.

4   Return the dough to the bowl and cover.

5   Allow the dough to rise for 8 hours or overnight.

6   When you're ready to assemble your rolls, preheat your oven to 350 degrees.

7   Oil a 9 x 13-inch pan.

8   In a small bowl, mix the cinnamon and brown sugar.

9   Place the dough onto a lightly floured surface.

10 Roll the dough out to approximately a 16 x 30-inch rectangle.

11 If making pumpkin cinnamon rolls, spread your puree across the entire surface of the dough.

12 Spread the melted butter on the dough so that the entire surface is covered with butter.

13 Sprinkle the cinnamon and brown sugar filling all the way to the edges of the dough.

14 Starting at one end of the 16-inch side, begin rolling the dough into a log. Be sure to keep the roll tight.

15 Using a pastry cutter, cut the dough into 1½ inch pieces.

16 Arrange the rolls in the pan.

17 Cover and let rise for 2 hours.

18 Bake at 350 degrees for 20 to 30 minutes.

19 While your rolls are baking, mix the ingredients for the icing in a mixing bowl.

20 Allow the cinnamon rolls to cool slightly before spreading the icing.

21 Enjoy!

YIELDS · 15-18 cinnamon rolls

CARROT CAKE

Macey

My husband's favorite dessert is carrot cake, so I knew that I had to master this recipe. My carrot cake is a labor of love, but it is so very worth it. He requests it for his birthday every year, and my son is obsessed with this dessert as well. Their birthdays are 11 days apart so, in the month of January, I make two of these one after the other (and yes, we eat two 9 x 13-inch baking dishes of it within that time frame)! This was even my son's smash cake for his first birthday! My husband and I have a deal, though. He grates the carrots for me because it truly makes a difference to grate by hand versus using a food processor, but whew, is it a workout! So, he gladly volunteers for that task because he knows the reward to his taste buds will be more than worth it!

PREP TIME · 20 minutes

COOK TIME · 50-60 minutes

Cake

- 2 cups granulated sugar
- 1 cup extra virgin olive oil
- 3 eggs, room temperature
- 1 cup unsweetened applesauce
- ½ cup sourdough discard
- 1 teaspoon vanilla extract
- 2 cups all-purpose flour
- 2 teaspoons ground cinnamon
- 2 teaspoons baking soda
- ¼ teaspoon salt
- ½ teaspoon ground ginger
- ¼ teaspoon ground nutmeg
- ¼ teaspoon ground cloves
- 3 cups carrots, finely shredded
- 2 cups walnuts, finely chopped in a food processor and divided

Frosting

- 6 ounces cream cheese, softened
- ½ cup butter, softened
- 3 cups powdered sugar, sifted
- 2 teaspoons vanilla extract
- ½ teaspoon salt
- Avocado oil cooking spray

1   Preheat your oven to 350 degrees.

2   Prepare a 9 x 13-inch baking dish by spraying the bottom and sides with avocado oil cooking spray.

3   Line with parchment paper if you want to easily remove it from the baking dish later.

4   In a stand mixer, combine the sugar, olive oil, eggs, applesauce, sourdough starter, and vanilla.

5   Mix on medium speed for about 2 minutes, until it is all combined well.

6   In a large mixing bowl, whisk together the flour, cinnamon, baking soda, salt, ginger, nutmeg, and cloves.

7   Add your carrots to your wet mixture.

8   Add the dry ingredients to the wet mixture and stir until just combined.

9   Add 1 cup of walnuts to your batter.

10 Pour the cake batter into the prepared dish and smooth out to make sure it's even in the pan.

11 Bake the cake at 350 degrees for 50 to 60 minutes or until a toothpick inserted in the center comes out clean.

12 Cool the cake completely.

13 In a stand mixer, add the softened cream cheese and butter and mix until it is fluffy, about 3 to 4 minutes.

14 Add in the powdered sugar, vanilla, and salt.

15 Mix on medium speed until combined and fluffy.

16 When your cake is completely cooled, cover with frosting, and sprinkle the remaining cup of walnuts over the cake.

YIELDS · One 9 x 13-inch carrot cake

DRESSINGS, DIPS & SEASONINGS

"True hospitality consists of giving the best of yourself to your guests."

— ELEANOR ROOSEVELT

Store bought dressings, dips, and seasonings certainly are convenient, but they are not always the healthiest since they are full of additives and preservatives. We have shared with you some of our favorite homemade creations to help offer you some cleaner options. They take very little time to prepare and taste so good! Enjoy!

217

SWEET AND SAVORY FRENCH DRESSING

Karen

The cooks of my mom's generation made French dressing with a can of tomato soup. I love French dressing, but I came up with a different recipe that is even more tasty! One of our staple salads uses this dressing with spring mix lettuce blend, cherry tomatoes, cucumber, purple onion, pickled beets, black olives, feta cheese, and toasted pine nuts. Such a refreshing meal starter.

PREP TIME · 10 minutes

- ⅔ cup apple cider vinegar
- ⅔ cup catsup
- ¾ cup sugar
- ½ teaspoon ground ginger
- 1 tablespoon prepared yellow mustard
- ½ teaspoon paprika
- 1 teaspoon salt
- 1¼ teaspoons black pepper
- ⅔ cup light olive oil
- 3 tablespoons finely chopped white or yellow onion

Hospitality Hack

Save unused dressing packets from restaurant salads in your refrigerator. Then, when you have company over, place the various packets in a small bowl to offer alongside whatever bottles of dressings you have out for the salad. This way guests can have several options from which to choose.

INSTRUCTIONS

1 Place all the ingredients in a blender and blend on high for 30 to 60 seconds.

2 Store in the refrigerator for up to 10 days.

YIELDS · About 2 ½ cups

UNCLE BO'S HONEY MUSTARD

Karen

My sister-in-law and brother-in-law, Erin and Bo, owned a bed and breakfast for years in Lake Worth, Florida called The Mango Inn. *Anything they made in the kitchen was fit for a top-rated cooking show. The first time I ever heard of honey mustard dressing was long before it was popular. Bo made some for my husband and me from scratch when we were visiting them after we first married and I've been using his recipe ever since.*

PREP TIME · 5 minutes

- 2 cups mayonnaise (not reduced-fat)
- ¼ cup honey
- ¼ red wine vinegar
- 1 tablespoon Dijon mustard
- 2 tablespoons fresh parsley, finely minced

INSTRUCTIONS

1   Combine all ingredients in a small bowl.

2   Store in the refrigerator in a covered glass container for up to 10 days.

YIELDS · About 2 ½ cups

Each of you should use whatever gift you have received to serve others, as faithful
stewards of God's grace in its various forms.

1 PETER 4:10

CAESAR DRESSING

Macey

On our honeymoon, my husband and I ate at Red Lobster, and I asked to eat there for two reasons. One, my dad had given us a Red Lobster gift card that he'd had in his wallet for ages as a wedding present (HAHA!), and two, because I love their Caesar salad. It is my absolute favorite along with the Cobb salad at Red Robin. If I'm eating a salad at a restaurant, those are the two options that you'll find in front of me. This is my personal twist on this classic dressing!

PREP TIME · 5 minutes

- ¼ cup mayonnaise
- ¼ cup spicy mayonnaise (see *Spicy Mayonnaise* recipe on page 226)
- 1½ teaspoon anchovy paste
- 1½ tablespoon olive oil
- 2 to 3 tablespoons lemon juice
- 1½ teaspoon spicy brown mustard
- 1 tablespoon Worcestershire sauce
- ½ teaspoon black pepper
- Salt, to taste
- 3 cloves garlic, finely minced
- ¼ cup sour cream
- ½ cup finely grated parmesan cheese

INSTRUCTIONS

1 In a mixing bowl, add mayonnaises, anchovy paste, olive oil, lemon juice, mustard, Worcestershire sauce, pepper, salt, and garlic and stir.

2 Whisk in sour cream and Parmesan cheese.

3 Place in a sealed jar in the refrigerator until serving.

YIELDS · About 1 ½ cups

CREAMY PARMESAN ITALIAN DRESSING

Karen

I made this dressing up after tasting something similar at a local Italian restaurant. It has a classic Italian flavor with a creamy, cool base. Dollop it on any leafy green salad to pair with one of our Italian dishes such as one of the lasagnas or spaghetti pie.

PREP TIME · 10 minutes

- 1 cup mayonnaise (not reduced fat)
- ½ cup sour cream
- ½ cup red wine vinegar
- 2 teaspoons sugar
- 1 tablespoon plus 1 teaspoon fresh lemon juice
- ½ cup olive oil
- 1½ teaspoons onion powder
- 1 teaspoon garlic powder
- ½ teaspoon dried oregano
- ½ teaspoon dried basil
- ½ teaspoon dried thyme
- ½ teaspoon dried rosemary
- ½ teaspoon dried marjoram
- 3 tablespoons fresh parsley
- ½ cup grated parmesan cheese

INSTRUCTIONS

1 Whisk all the ingredients together in a small bowl until well blended.

2 Store in the refrigerator in a covered container for up to 10 days.

YIELDS · About 2 ½ cups

PESTO SAUCE

Macey

This past summer, I had such an abundance of herbs like basil and parsley. Our new home in Tennessee has the perfect herb-growing spot, and my plants just exploded. I needed a recipe to use up my abundant harvest, and so, I came up with my spin on a pesto recipe. In addition, I have a couple of friends with nut allergies, and I wanted them to be able to enjoy this as well! So, this recipe is nut-allergy friendly!

PREP TIME · 15 minutes
COOK TIME · 5 minutes

- 4 tablespoons lemon juice
- 2 garlic cloves
- ½ teaspoon salt
- ¼ teaspoon black pepper
- 2 cups basil
- 2 cups parsley
- ½ cup olive oil
- ½ cup Parmesan

SOUL SOOTHER

Gardening can improve our mood and can decrease stress and anxious feelings. We experience gratification when we tend to and harvest our gardens. Routines of watering our plants can also create a rhythm of peace that eases our stress.

INSTRUCTIONS

1. Blend all ingredients in a food processor or blender until desired consistency.

2. Store in a tightly sealed glass jar for your pesto to last longer.

3. Multiply the ingredients as required if needing to make a larger batch.

YIELDS · About 4-5 ounces

BUTTERMILK BLUE CHEESE DRESSING

Karen

The family I grew up in did not eat gourmet type foods. My mom was a vintage homemaker who made meat and potatoes, lots of casseroles, and scrumptious from-scratch desserts. If we had a salad, we ate it with French or Thousand Island dressing or occasionally the Kraft™ creamy cucumber store-bought variety. I never tasted blue cheese dressing until I married into the Ehman family. I found it to be not only quite fancy, but quite delicious too! Here is our go-to recipe.

PREP TIME · 5 minutes

- 1 cup full-fat buttermilk (not reduced fat)
- 1 cup mayonnaise (not reduced fat)
- 2 tablespoons fresh lemon juice
- ½ teaspoon Worcestershire sauce
- 2 garlic cloves, finely minced
- ½ teaspoon salt
- ¼ teaspoon black pepper
- 3 ounces blue cheese, coarsely crumbled

INSTRUCTIONS

1   A medium bowl, blend all the ingredients but the blue cheese until smooth.

2   Fold in the blue cheese crumbles.

3   Store in the refrigerator in a covered container for up to 10 days.

YIELDS · About 3 cups

PAPA PAT'S HOUSE DRESSING

Karen

At his restaurant, Pat's Pantry *in Lansing, Michigan, my dad was well known for his Friday night fish fry dinner, his homemade coleslaw, his colorful ambrosia fruit salad, and most importantly, his famous house salad dressing. This is unlike any dressing I've ever tasted. Very decadent, but entirely delicious.*

PREP TIME · 10 minutes

- 1 cup evaporated milk
- ¼ cup white vinegar
- 1 cup salad dressing (not mayonnaise)
- ½ cup sugar
- ¼ cup white onion, grated
- 2 tablespoons celery seed
- ¾ teaspoon salt
- 1 teaspoon black pepper
- 5 hard boiled eggs, chopped

INSTRUCTIONS

1   In a medium bowl, blend all the ingredients but the eggs.

2   Gently fold in the eggs.

3   Store in the refrigerator in a covered container for up to 10 days.

YIELDS · About 3 cups

SPICY MAYONNAISE

Macey

Spicy mayonnaise is another convenience item whose price had me frowning recently. We love it and eat a lot of it in our home, but sometimes we put it back on the shelf until next time or unless there is a sale. This recipe is the solution to that problem. We can find these ingredients in bulk for lower prices at our local grocery store! Just multiple the ingredients accordingly if you need a larger batch!

PREP TIME · 5 minutes

- 1 cup mayonnaise
- 2 tablespoons sriracha sauce
- 1 teaspoon paprika
- 1 teaspoon garlic powder
- 1 teaspoon onion powder

INSTRUCTIONS

1   Add all ingredients to a bowl and stir well to combine.

2   Store in a jar with a lid or use immediately!

YIELDS · 1 cup

RANCH SEASONING MIX

Karen

We Midwesterners love our ranch dressing. I couldn't keep enough in the house when my daughter, Kenna, was a teen. She and her friends didn't just put it on salad, they also dipped slices of pizza in it, or homemade bread sticks, or chicken wings, or they put it on top of baked potatoes. Anything, really! However, prepared ranch dressings aren't always the healthiest. Use this seasoning to make your own dressing or dip.

PREP TIME · 5 minutes

- 2 tablespoons dried parsley
- 2 tablespoons dried basil
- 2 tablespoons dried oregano
- 1 tablespoon dried thyme
- 1 tablespoon dried rosemary
- 1 tablespoon dried marjoram
- 1 tablespoon plus 2 teaspoons dried minced garlic
- 1 tablespoon cracked black pepper
- 2 teaspoons salt

INSTRUCTIONS

1   Mix all ingredients until well incorporated.

2   Store in an airtight container.

To make dressing: Combine 2 tablespoons of the seasoning mix with ⅓ cup mayonnaise (not reduced fat), and ⅓ cup whole milk and whisk to combine.

To make dip: Combine 2½ tablespoons of the mix with ⅓ cup sour cream.

YIELDS · About ½ cup

TACO SEASONING MIX

Macey

When prices started to rise at the grocery store, I looked for ways to make my own versions of many of the convenience items that I used to buy. One of these items was taco seasoning. It's amazing how the price adds up when buying multiple packs! I can make the same amount for much cheaper at home, and my husband says the flavor is much better!

PREP TIME · 5 minutes

- 1 tablespoon chili powder
- 1½ teaspoons ground cumin
- 1 teaspoon salt
- 1 teaspoon black pepper
- ½ teaspoon smoked paprika
- ¼ teaspoon garlic powder
- ¼ teaspoon onion powder
- ¼ teaspoon crushed red pepper flakes
- ¼ teaspoon dried oregano
- 1 tablespoon brown sugar

INSTRUCTIONS

1   Mix all ingredients until well incorporated.

2   Store in an airtight container or use immediately to season your favorite Latin American dish.

3   Use about 1½ tablespoons of seasoning mix per pound of meat, or more to taste.

YIELDS · Enough to season 2 pounds of meat

ITALIAN SEASONING MIX

Karen

Whether making your own pasta sauce from scratch or adding this mix to olive oil, ground sea salt, and cracked pepper to dip fresh bread into, this recipe is so easy and much cheaper than buying premade.

PREP TIME · 5 minutes

- 2 tablespoons dried parsley
- 2 tablespoons dried basil
- 2 tablespoons dried oregano
- 1 tablespoon dried thyme
- 1 tablespoon dried rosemary
- 1 tablespoon dried marjoram
- 1 tablespoon dried minced garlic

INSTRUCTIONS

1. Mix all ingredients until well incorporated.
2. Store in an airtight container or use immediately to season your favorite Italian dishes.

YIELDS · About ½ cup

About the Authors

KAREN EHMAN is a *New York Times* bestselling author, a sought-after speaker, a contributing writer for Proverbs 31 Ministries *Encouragement for Today* online devotions, and a teacher in the *First 5* Bible study app. She has written 20 books and Bible studies including *Keep It Shut: What to Say, How to Say It, and When to Say Nothing at All* and the 2020 ECPA devotional book of the year *Settle My Soul: 100 Quiet Moments to Meet with Jesus*. She is a graduate of Spring Arbor University with a major in Social Science.

Karen has been featured on TODAY Parenting, Redbook.com, Foxnews.com, Crosswalk.com, YouVersion.com, and is a monthly columnist for *HomeLife* Magazine. Her passion is to help women live their priorities as they reflect the gospel to a watching world. She is married to her college sweetheart, Todd, and is the mother of six children: three biological and three in-laws by marriage—although she forgets which ones are which. But her most treasured role is being Grandma Kit to the adorable Jasper Ridge. She enjoys collecting vintage aqua and pink Pyrex kitchenware, and spending her days feeding the many people who gather around her mid-century dining table to process life and enjoy her county fair blue-ribbon winning cooking. You can visit her website at karenehman.com, or find her on Instagram at @karenehman, Facebook at @OfficialKarenEhman, or Pinterest at @karenehmanofficial.

MACEY EHMAN received her Master of Education and Education Specialist degrees in School Counseling from Valdosta State University in 2016 and 2018 respectively. She is a school counselor licensed in the states of Georgia and Michigan and currently practices in Georgia. She is also a National Certified Counselor as well as a Licensed Professional Counselor in the state of Michigan. At the writing of this book, she is seeking the same license in the state of Georgia.

She lives on a small homestead on the banks of the Ocoee River near the Georgia/Tennessee border with her husband, Mitchell, her son, Jasper, and her three farm dogs, Aspen, Smoky, and Luna. She is passionate about approaching mental health from a Biblical, holistic, and cognitive-behavioral standpoint, integrating her knowledge of physical health, emotional health, and spiritual health to produce optimal growth and healing, Lord willing. In her free time, she enjoys creating new recipes in the kitchen and cooking and baking for her family and friends. She seeks to make everyone that walks through her door feel loved and welcomed. You can follow along with her counseling pages on Facebook and Instagram at @maceyehmanpllc and her homestead adventures on both sites at @thefarmonfederal.

Made in the USA
Middletown, DE
11 December 2023

45331059R00128